Habsburg Treasures: Renaissance Tapestries

from the Kunsthistorisches Museum, Vienna

Dr. Katja Schmitz-von Ledebur

INTERNATIONAL ARTS & ARTISTS, WASHINGTON, D.C.

 IA&A is a non-profit organization dedicated to increasing cross-cultural understanding and exposure to the arts internationally through exhibitions, programs and services to artists, arts institutions, and the public.

Habsburg Treasures: Renaissance Tapestries from the Kunsthistorisches Museum, Vienna is developed by the Kunsthistorisches Museum Wien, Kunstkammer and is organized for tour by International Arts & Artists, Washington, DC.

Exhibition Dates:

The Norton Museum of Art, West Palm Beach, FL
January 16, 2010 – April 11, 2010

The Columbia Museum of Art, Columbia, SC
May 21, 2010 – September 19, 2010

The John and Mable Ringling Museum of Art, Sarasota, FL
October 7, 2010 – December 30, 2010

Library of Congress Cataloging-in-Publication Data

Schmitz-von Ledebur, Katja.
Habsburg Treasures : Renaissance Tapestries from the Kunsthistorisches Museum, Vienna / Katja Schmitz-von Ledebur.
p. cm.
Published on the occasion of an exhibition held at the Norton Museum of Art, West Palm Beach, Fla., Jan. 16-Apr. 11, 2010; the Columbia Museum of Art, Columbia, S.C., May 21-Sept. 19, 2010; and the John and Mable Ringling Museum of Art, Sarasota, Fla., Oct. 7-Dec. 30, 2010.
ISBN 978-0-9767102-8-8
1. Tapestry, Flemish--Belgium--Brussels--History--16th century--Exhibitions. 2. Tapestry, Renaissance--Belgium--Brussels--Exhibitions. 3. Romulus, King of Rome--Art--Exhibitions. 4. Remus (Twin of Romulus, King of Rome)--Art--Exhibitions. 5. Habsburg, House of--Art collections--Exhibitions. 6. Tapestry--Austria--Vienna--Exhibitions. 7. Kunsthistorisches Museum Wien--Exhibitions. I. Norton Museum of Art. II. Columbia Museum of Art. III. John and Mable Ringling Museum of Art. IV. Title. V. Title: Renaissance tapestries from the Kunsthistorisches Museum, Vienna.
NK3055.A1S36 2010
746.39493'07443613--dc22
2009049326

Produced by International Arts & Artists, 9 Hillyer Court, NW, Washington, DC, 20008
www.artsandartists.org
Production Editors and Managers: Marlene Rothacker and Nicole Forrest
Copy Editor: Penny Kiser
Translations by Dirk Holger and Sabrina Ratzer
Designed by Katie Dahl Laux, International Arts & Artists' Design Studio
This book was typeset in Goudy Old Style and printed by Balmar, Inc.

Front cover: *Remus Captured and Brought before Amulius* (detail), ca 1560-70, Scenes from the *Saga of Romulus and Remus* series, Brussels, Workshop of Frans Geubels (page 28)

Back cover: *Romulus and Remus Suckled by a She-wolf* (detail), ca 1560-70, Scenes from the *Saga of Romulus and Remus* series, Brussels, Workshop of Frans Geubels (page 24)

Contents

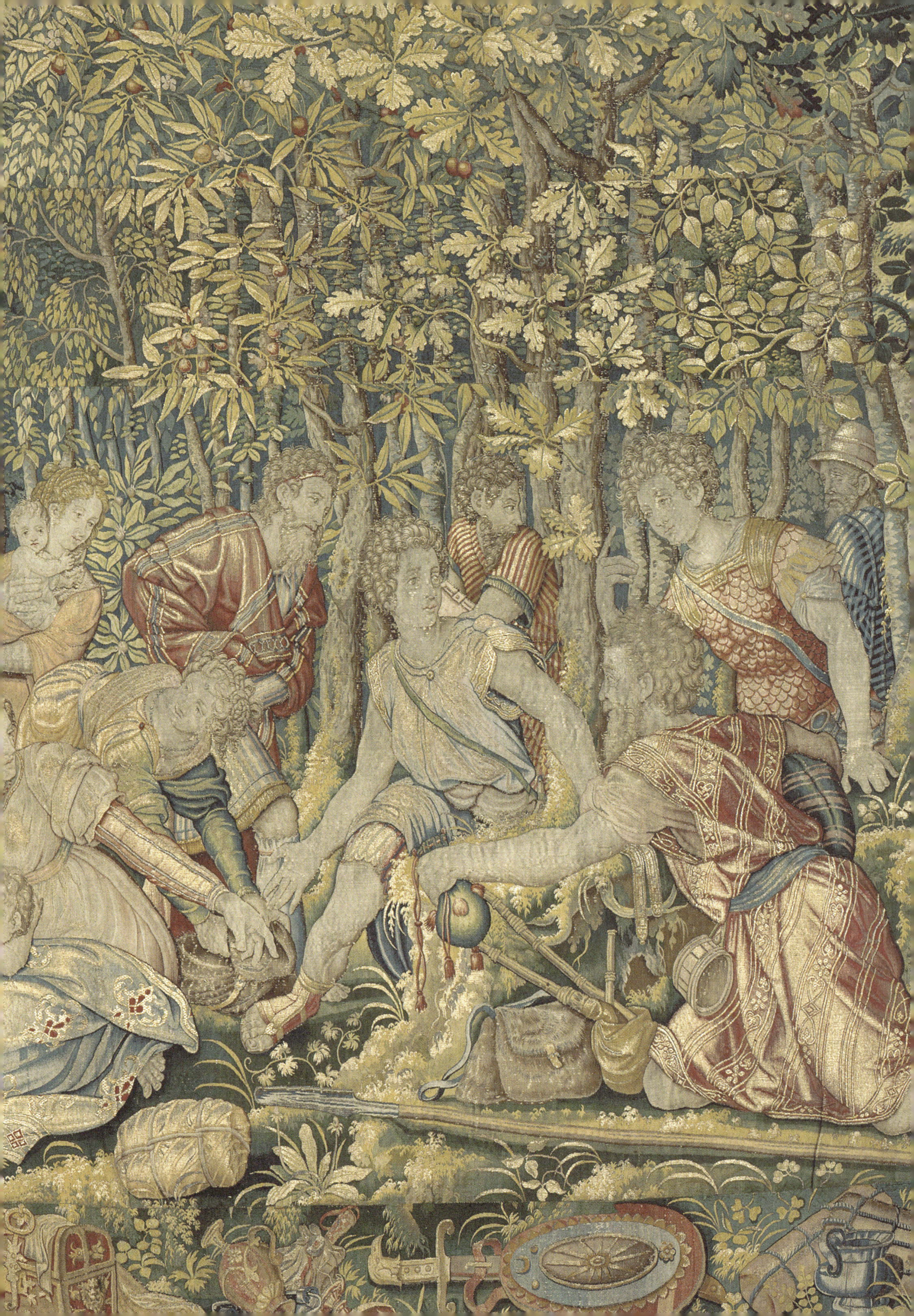

Preface

It has been a great honor to collaborate with the Kunsthistorisches Museum in Vienna. This renowned Austrian cultural institution, with one of the world's finest collections of Renaissance tapestries, is now sharing these treasures with American audiences for an exclusive three-city tour. The Kunsthistorisches Museum also took great care in undertaking the restoration of these tapestries especially for this tour. We are deeply indebted to Dr. Katja Schmitz von Ledebur, curator of this exhibition and curator of the collection of sculpture and decorative arts (Kunstkammer) and of the secular and ecclesiastical treasury, for allowing this precious collection to travel to the United States as well as for her contributing essays to this exhibition catalogue.

We thank Dirk Holger for bringing these works to our attention and for his ardent efforts in the development of the exhibition. Mr. Holger also translated this exhibition catalogue into English with assistance by Sabrina Ratzer.

Within International Arts & Artists, we acknowledge the assistance of the director of our Traveling Exhibition Service, Marlene Rothacker; Nicole Forrest and her predecessor Amanda Cane, the senior exhibitions managers who arranged the tour; and Elizabeth Wilson, assistant director and head registrar, for organizing the loans and bringing the works to the U.S. We also thank Katie Laux, IA&A's Design Studio director and designer of the *Habsburg Treasures* catalogue.

For the benefit of all,
David Furchgott, President
International Arts & Artists

Left: *The Twins Sharing the Loot* (detail), ca 1560-70
Scenes from the *Saga of Romulus and Remus* series
Brussels, Workshop of Frans Geubels (page 27)

Foreword by Ambassador Matthysen

Dear Reader:

This exhibition presents tapestries woven in Brussels, which were inspired by the story of the founding of Rome and whose permanent home is a museum in Vienna. What a wonderful example of the commingling of European cultures!

Americans who have the opportunity to view this traveling exhibition will be reminded that Flanders was one of the great economic and artistic centers of Northern Europe from the end of the Middle Ages through the 18th century. Thousands of artists, designers and weavers worked in Brussels where the art of tapestry weaving reached its zenith in the 16th century. Tapestry workshops created sets of tapestries for patrons and customers intent on decorating (and insulating) their homes with these "mobile frescoes," as they have been described. Oftentimes these tapestries told a story, such as that of Romulus and Remus selected for this exhibition. The stories not only demonstrate the renewed interest in classical Rome during the Renaissance, but also contain political references and metaphors of special meaning to the tapestries' owners, in this case the Habsburg family.

Congratulations to Dirk Holger for initiating this exhibition and to International Arts & Artists for organizing its tour in the United States. My thanks go also to the Kunsthistorisches Museum for lending these remarkable tapestries which bear witness to Belgium's artistic heritage.

Jan Matthysen
Ambassador of Belgium to the United States

Foreword by Ambassador Prosl

Austrian Embassy
Washington

Dear Visitors,

It is a particular pleasure for me to welcome you to the exhibition *Habsburg Treasures: Renaissance Tapestries from the Kunsthistorisches Museum, Vienna*. The tapestry collection of the Kunsthistorisches Museum is regarded worldwide as one of the most magnificent of its kind. The exhibition will convince you of the outstanding quality of the pieces shown as well as remind you of the predilection for the arts of the Habsburgs over the centuries, since the series of tapestries owned now by the Austrian state emerged from the possessions of the former imperial family. For the first time, the exhibition provides U.S. audiences a rare opportunity to view these precious wall hangings that have been recently restored. Austria is proud to be able to share these treasures with you.

I wish to thank all the people involved in making this exhibition possible, first of all the staff from the Kunsthistorisches Museum and the staff from the three U.S. museums where the tapestries will be shown, the Norton Museum of Art in West Palm Beach, Florida, the Columbia Museum of Art in South Carolina and the John and Mable Ringling Museum of Art in Sarasota, Florida. Particular thanks go to Dirk Holger, the initiator of the exhibition who had the brilliant idea to bring this exquisite selection of tapestries to the U.S. through International Arts & Artists, Washington, D.C., who is coordinating all tour efforts including this catalogue.

I wish you all a very pleasant and exciting visit and congratulate you for being part of a once-in-a-lifetime chance to indulge in these textile splendors.

Christian Prosl
Ambassador of Austria to the United States

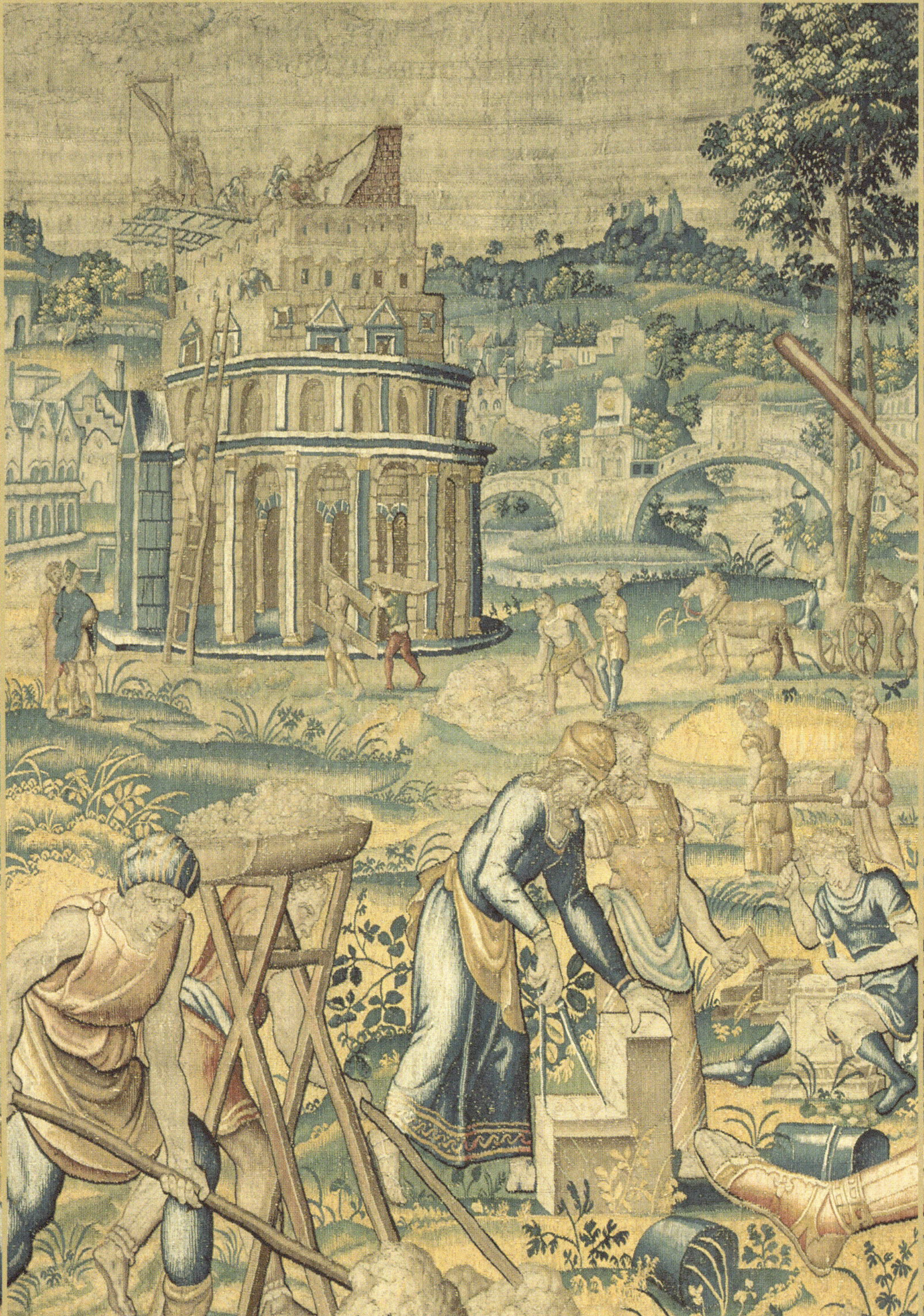

Introduction

Dr. Katja Schmitz-von Ledebur

The tapestry collection of the Kunsthistorisches Museum is considered as one of the most magnificent of its kind with regard to its richness and artistic importance. These Habsburg tapestries are among one of the world's most significant collections which include the holdings in the Royal Palace in Madrid, those of the Mobilier National in Paris and the former possessions of the Medici Family in Florence. As with the collection from Madrid, which came from the Gardemeuble of the Spanish crown and the collection from Paris, which came from that of the French crown, the tapestry collection from the state of Austria arose from the possessions of Habsburg. After the collapse of the monarchy, the collection was donated to the Kunsthistorisches Museum.

With the Collection of Sculpture and Decorative Arts at the Kunsthistorisches Museum under renovation, audiences have the opportunity to view several of the collection's most precious wall hangings as they tour the United States. The exhibition includes six recently restored tapestries from the belongings of Emperor Matthias (1557-1619).

These wall hangings, from the famous workshop of Frans Geubels in Brussels, depict one of the most popular topics of 16th-century Flemish tapestry: historical scenes of the remarkable founding of Rome. The fact that tapestries featuring the same subject were owned by the King of France, Francis I (1494–1547), and the Emperor of the Holy Roman Empire, Rudolf II (1552-1612), underlines the popularity of this subject.

The series shows in eloquent images the eventful life of the twins Romulus and Remus, grandchildren of King Numitor, who was dethroned by his brother in Alba Longa. The series starts with the birth of the brothers who were abandoned in a wicker basket on the Tiber river. They were rescued and suckled by a she-wolf until they were found by a shepherd and his wife who then raised them. As young men, Romulus and Remus defeated Amulius, helped their grandfather back to his legitimate throne, and finally founded the city of Rome.

Two of the tapestries from the Romulus and Remus series had to be sold in 1953, which is why the museum only has six of the original eight tapestries from the series. However, the Kunsthistorisches Museum has another tapestry series depicting the history of Romulus and Remus, which stems from the heritage of Emperor Franz I (1708-1765), Maria Theresia's husband. The Franz I series is dated slightly later and the workmanship is not as precise, but they were created according to the same drafts as the Habsburg tapestries, and provide substitutes for the two missing tapestries. This circumstance also offers the opportunity to show that popular subjects were issued several times in the workshops of Brussels and were made with different techniques and according to the commissioner's preferences. Both series testify to Flemish stylistic innovations and the influences of the Italian Renaissance during the second decade of the 16th century. With these two series of tapestries the Kunsthistorisches Museum has without a doubt some of the most significant examples of the production of tapestries in Brussels in the 16th century with no less than Habsburg provenance.

Left: *The Founding of Rome* (detail), ca 1565-70
Scenes from the *Saga of Romulus and Remus* series
Brussels (page 32)

The Production of a Tapestry

Tapestries[1] are created with a technique called tapestry weaving, a method related to both weaving and knitting. As in weaving, tapestry weaving shares the stretched warp threads and the weft that is inserted at right angles to the threads. The technique of plain weaving is to weave the weft yarn back and forth into the whole fabric. When using the tapestry weaving technique, the colored weft is only inserted as far at the color field extends according to the design.

When and where this technique was first introduced cannot be clearly verified. It had been known for a long time that it was possible to produce a fabric by crossing yarns; the appliance of different colors already alludes to the technique of weaving. It can be assumed that the technique of weaving was developed simultaneously at different places. We have, for example, evidence of coptic weaving from the Nile Delta and from the Nile Valley.

The weavers found their field of activity—after first being consulted for the production of clothing—in creating monumental textile images, such as the production of tapestries. The creation of such a wall hanging normally takes place in three steps. In the first cycle a design (*petit patron*) is presented. The choice of the subject results either directly from the artist or the commissioner. Under the guidelines of this design sketch a full-scale colored pattern, known as the cartoon, or preparatory drawing or painting for a tapestry (*grand patron*), is made in a second cycle. This cartoon is mostly colored with opaque or watercolors and only seldomly with oil paint. In this step the rough draft is realized in exact forms, which serve the weaver as their direction. The quality of this pattern is definitive for the appearance of the final product. Already in the 15th century, in the prime of the French and Dutch weaving ateliers, the profession of the painter of cartoons became an autonomous and important discipline.

For the production of the relatively large tapestries, a special loom with a device to stretch the parallelly aligned warps was developed. In these yarns, which lie closely together, the colored weft is inserted at a right angle (image 1). During this process the weft lies alternately above and below the warps. The weft that is already inserted is regularly stroked with a comb, i.e. beaten down, so that the warps are covered completely. Thus, the tapestry's pattern is constituted exclusively by the weft. The tapestry loom's nature has changed little since its development. Depictions of forerunners to high and low warp looms can be found in Egyptian wall paintings and Greek vases.

Although the warps are not visible to the naked eye, they admittedly are apparent in the form of slender ridges on the textile's surface. When working with a high warp loom (*haute lisse*), the weaver sits in front of the warps as if sitting in front of a wall, since these are stretched vertically before him (image 2). He traces the draft's outlines onto the warps with black chalk, which is not transparent through the yarn's bright colors, and hangs up the cartoon in the actual size behind him to always be able to check his work. On the low warp loom (*basse lisse*), however, the warps are spanned horizontally. The weaver positions the cartoon, which is rolled or cut into stripes, under the warps and can glance through the warps at the cartoon to check his work. The difficulty with working with a low warp loom is that the weaver produces the tapestry design in reverse, only seeing the back of the tapestry. That way it is easy to understand why tapestries created in the *basse-lisse* method depict the draft as well as the cartoon invertedly.[2]

The weaver's impact on the artistic expression of the tapestry is the most essential part of creating a tapestry. His task is not only to insert the weft alternately over and under the warps but also to bring the cartoon's rich details about the color into a harmonic accord, as well as to translate the nuances and design into the textile medium. The weaver's virtuosity and attention to detail define the quality of a tapestry just as much as the design and the cartoon.

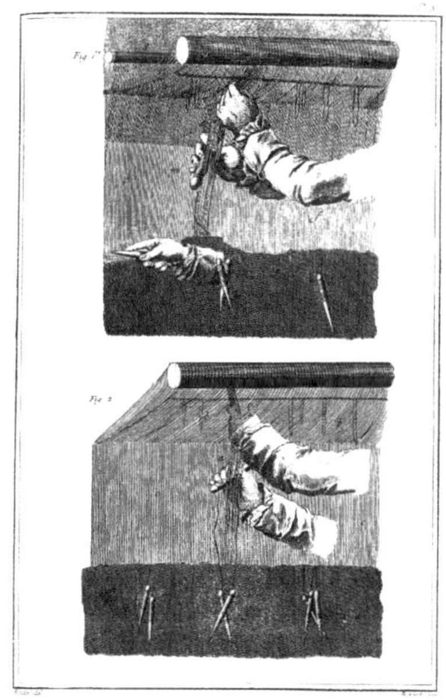

1 Denis Diderot: Encyclopédie

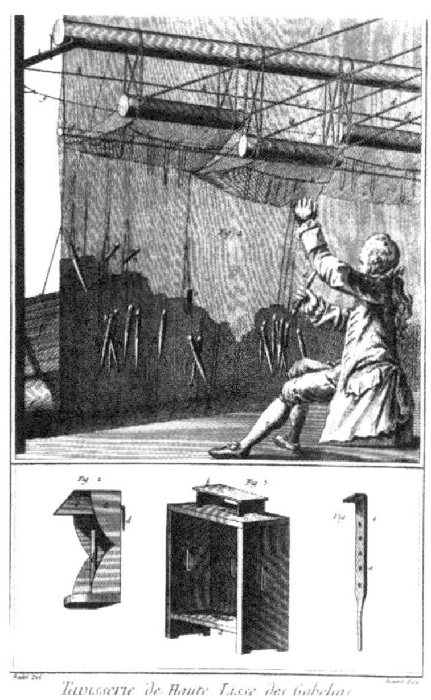

2 Denis Diderot: Encyclopédie

1 The word tapestry derives from the Greek word ταπης (*tapes*) and the Latin word *tapetum* (carpet, blanket, paper hangings).

2 A second aspect complicates the weaver's work both at the high and the low warp loom. As a general rule, tapestries were wider than high. For economical reasons it became the custom to produce the design tilted over, i.e. rotated by 90°. The warp looms at which several weavers worked simultaneously in most cases were consequently more slender and space-saving.

Design of the Tapestry Border

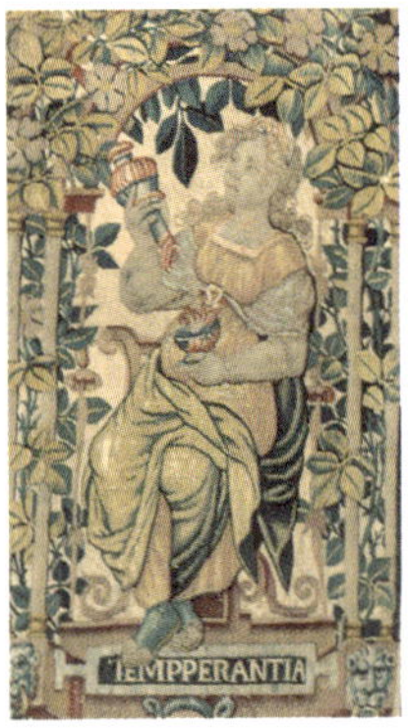

1 Personification of the Seven Virtues: Temperantia (Temperance)

The two sets of Romulus and Remus tapestries in Vienna are framed by two different borders. The border of the two tapestries *Romulus Delivers the Head of Amulius* (page 31 and image 3 below) and the *Founding of Rome* (page 32) that belong to the series that comes from the estate of Emperor Franz I is rendered more coarsely. These show in the upper horizontal border an inscription in Latin, framed by ornaments and masks, which explains the themes of each image. Between fruit and flower bouquets in the borders, the personification of the Seven Virtues are placed beneath pergolas (image 1).

The design for this border was not specifically made for the Vienna series. They already appeared in a popular tapestry series representing the Seven Virtues produced by the workshop of Frans Geubels. Here they round off the themes portrayed in the tapestries. Cartoons of these borders must have been stored in the studio of Frans Geubels and were readily available for use in the Romulus and Remus tapestry sets.

More lavish is the border of the second Vienna series (image 4) that formerly belonged to the Emperor Matthias (1557-1619). In the upper horizontal border cherubs hold panels with inscriptions in Latin that explain the content of each tapestry. In the lower left horizontal border Mars and Fama, and to the right Generosity and Justice, are depicted. Cartouches in the center of the lower horizontal borders show scenes from the mythological story of Hercules monochromatically (image 2). Except for one (Hercules and Atlas) they are all based on etchings by Heinrich Aldegrever (1502-1550), an important German etcher, painter and seal-maker of the Renaissance.

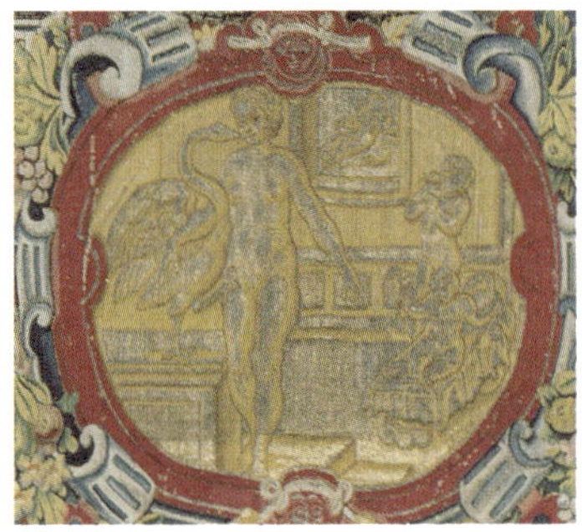

2 Scene from the Mythological Story of Hercules

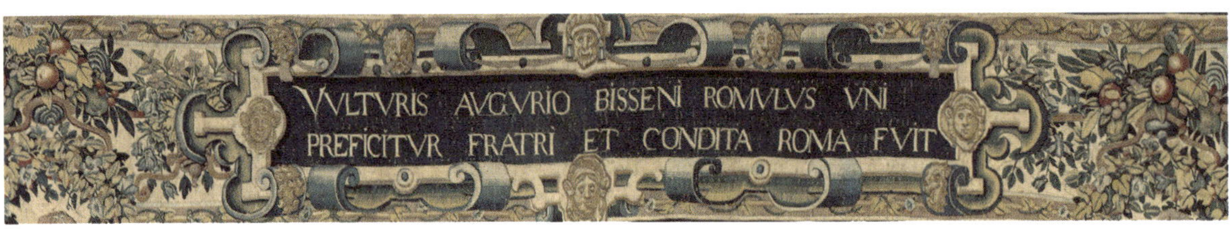

3 Upper horizontal border of *Romulus Delivers the Head of Amulius to Numitor*, from the first Vienna series from the Estate of Emperor Frans I (page 31)

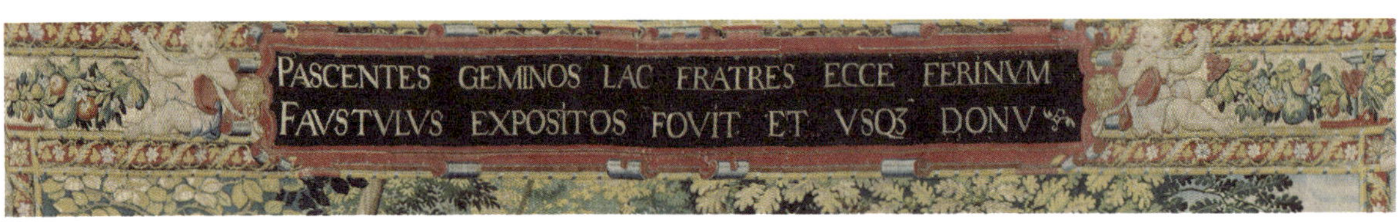

4 Upper horizontal border of *Romulus and Remus are Suckled by She-wolf*, from the second Vienna series that belonged to Emperor Matthias (page 24)

These etchings of a total of 13 episodes were first published in 1550. The portrayal of the deeds of Hercules alludes to the heroism of the twin brothers Romulus and Remus. Sometimes we even find direct parallels in the panels of the tapestries.

The borders show precisely rendered animals with inscriptions placed below them as well as ornate flowers and caryatides. Of the more than 20 images of animals, several appear numerous times while some appear only once in the borders of these tapestries. Worth mentioning is the ostrich in the tapestry *The Twins Sharing the Loot*, bearing this inscription: ALTA CERNENS TERRENA SPERNIT (image 5).

According to Physiologus, an early Christian compendium on animal symbolism, the ostrich waits for the appearance of the constellation of the Pleiade before laying eggs in the sand. The ostrich leaves the hatching entirely to the warmth of the sun. One can see in this motif a hint at the fate of the twin brothers Romulus and Remus, who were raised by the she-wolf and not by their mother Rhea Silvia.

The extensive iconography of these borders was also not intended for the Romulus and Remus series. It was probably made for the popular Cyrus tapestries in the collection of King Philip II of Spain, which were woven in the workshops of Frans Geubels and Jan van Tieghem. They were used at the funeral ceremonies for King Francis II of France in 1560 and therefore were produced before that year. The cartoons of the borders could have been used in the workshop of Frans Geubels and possibly reused for the Romulus and Remus tapestries. This circumstance indicates the dating of the Romulus and Remus tapestries after 1550, based on the Hercules cycle by Heinrich Aldegrever, which was published earlier.

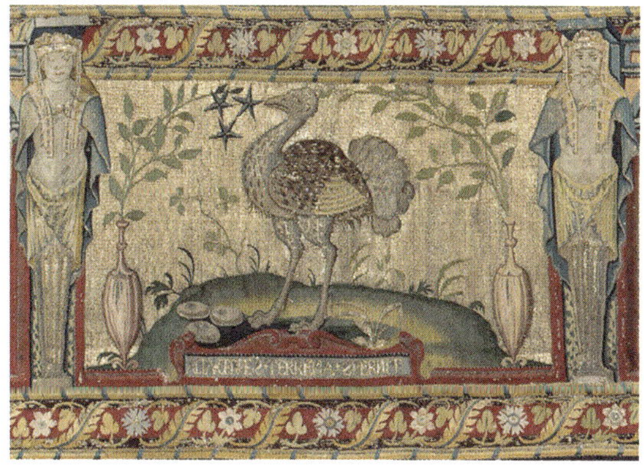

5 *The Twins Sharing the Loot* (detail), c. 1560 (page 27)

Conservation of the Romulus and Remus Tapestries

The production of a tapestry is quite costly and can only be performed by hand. As a rule, it took several years for a typical tapestry to be woven in the scale of the 16th century, although there were several weavers working simultaneously on the same loom. Experience shows that executing conservation also demands much time.

One such extensive project of the Restoration Studio of the Treasury was the conservation of the set of tapestries from the 16th century, *Scenes from the Saga of Romulus and Remus,* featured in this exhibition. The designs for this series came from the circle of Bernard van Orley (ca 1492-1542). In 1997, the Manufactory of de Wit in Mechelen (Belgium) applied a soft cleaning method for the set of six tapestries of the Kunsthistorisches Museum. This type of conservation method lasted, with some interruption, for several years.

Before conservation could begin, a detailed examination of the tapestries took place, followed by recording the content. The condition of the six tapestries, richly interwoven with gold threads, appeared mediocre.

Damaged parts were mainly found among the brown wools and the light-colored silks. In many portions the woolen warps lay open and were often torn. The tapestries also showed brittle seams and open slits. Borders and selvedges (edges of a tapestry) were shown to have more wear and tear than the main tapestry images.

During restoration, some old, improper repairs—which damaged the weaving—were taken out. Seams of slits were examined and eventually strengthened and fragile or defective parts were consolidated as well as missing warps and wefts replaced. About thirty square meters of the tapestry weaves were treated this way. The end of the conservation process was the complete lining of each tapestry with tried and tested textiles. The application of the lining took special care of the fragile parts of the weavings.

Restorers:
Ulrike Akbiyik-Messner, Andrea Antoniuk, Karin Hammerschmid, Eva-Maria Jerabek, Isabella Stehlik

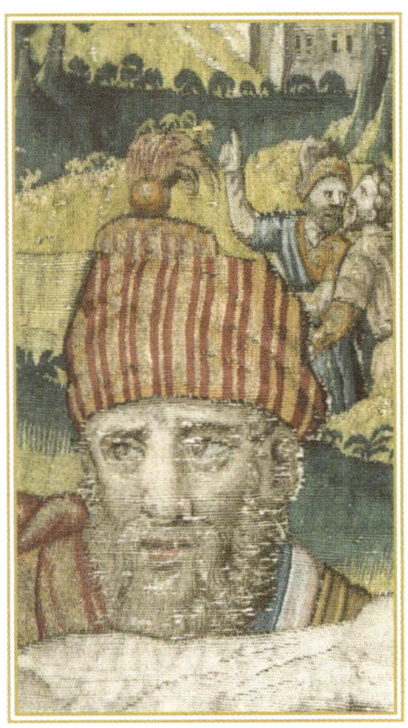

Before

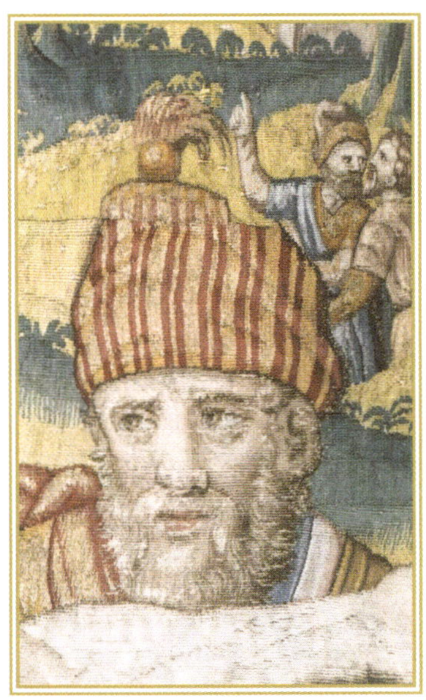

After

Remus Captured and Brought before Amulius (detail), ca 1560-70, Scenes from the *Saga of Romulus and Remus* series, Brussels, Workshop of Frans Geubels (page 28)

Tapestries Depicting the Story of Romulus and Remus

During the Renaissance, publications by historians such as Titus Livius helped renew interest in ancient Rome, and in particular, the story of the founding of Rome and the role of twin brothers Romulus and Remus. The story of Romulus and Remus became a beloved theme in the art of tapestry of the time. In these tapestries, produced as a series, the heroism of the brothers elevated them to the status of idols and identification figures for Renaissance rulers.

Around 1524, the Flemish painter Bernard van Orley (1492-1542) designed a set of Romulus and Remus tapestries (Munich, Graphische Sammlung) which was probably acquired by Henry VIII of England (1491-1547). We know of several tapestry sets created since then with similar themes, two of which are part of the Kunsthistorisches Museum collection in Vienna. The designers and prepatory design painters who painted for both series, in which the protagonists, dressed in period attire, tell the story of the twin brothers and the founding of Rome, remained unknown until recently.

The set executed in the finer weaving technique of the two Viennese sets is possibly identical to one mentioned in the 1587 last will and testament of Archduke Matthias (1557-1619), later the emperor of the Holy Roman Empire.

These tapestries are surely dated earlier than 1587. Evidence for the attribution of them to this exclusive provenance is the fact that they were produced with gold threads and therefore were more costly. Tapestries woven with metallic threads demonstrate their value and the financial power and status of the person who was able to afford them.

The designer of the Vienna tapestries used for inspiration a series from 1540 woven by the prestigious Brussels workshop of Willem de Pannemaker. Two panels of this set belong today to the collection of the Patrimonio Nacional in Madrid; four more are in private collections. These tapestries most likely belong to the set acquired in 1550 by the dealer Jan van de Walle for King Philip II of Spain. The designs were attributed to an artist in the circle of the Flemish painter Michiel van Coxcie (1499-1592), or the Italian Tommaso Vincidor (1493-1536), a painter in the circle of Raphael. Vincidor worked as a cartoon painter in the Netherlands from about 1521 to 1536.

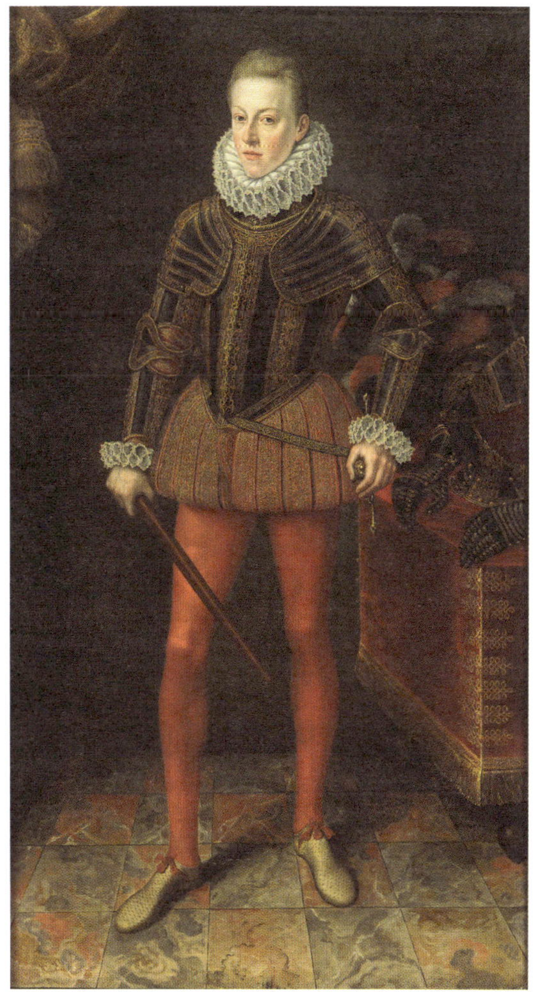

Matthias, Holy Roman Emperor (1557-1619)

We find the city mark of Brussels in the selvedge (edge on either side of a textile) as well as the initials "F" and "G," presumably standing for Frans Geubels whose workshop was active in Brussels between 1551 and 1577. Due to several ornamental cartouches in the borders, coming from a Hercules series of drawings (Munich, Graphische Sammlung), the entire tapestry series must be dated after 1550 when these drawings were first published and give us a terminus post quem.

All eight tapestries in this series contain an unusual feature: they all had at some point 40 centimeters added to their height, probably sometime still in the 16th century. They were cut horizontally in the upper zone and a separately woven strip, which expanded the composition in a highly skillful way, was added. Two panels of this Vienna set were sold in 1953 and now belong to the collection of the Toledo Museum of Art in Ohio.

In the second tapestry series of Vienna, with its representation of the legend of Romulus and Remus, the protagonists are set more dominantly in the foreground. Also, the rendering of the landscape is less detailed. This series also shows the initials "F" and "G," plus marks of two unidentified workshops. The complete set comes from the estate of Emperor Franz I (1708-1765). But for whom these tapestries produced in the 16th century were made or who acquired them initially, remains unknown.

Both tapestry series of Vienna tell in detail the story of the twin brothers Romulus and Remus and the founding of Rome. As mentioned, mythical themes from antiquity like this one were popular subjects during the Renaissance. In the selection of subjects for tapestry series their final purpose was most important. As prestigious symbols, they supported the status, reputation, respect and esteem of a person or emphasized the representational element of a ceremonial act. Therefore they had to be timeless and above all versatile. Both Vienna series fulfilled these requirements. Despite some open questions about the tapestries—especially the one concerning the designer(s)—they belong without any doubt to the most magnificent series of the 16th century. Particularly the set from the collection of Emperor Matthias (1557-1619), with its richly interwoven gold and silver threads, we can assume that they once decorated rooms of the highest demand for representation. The very fact that these tapestries were produced by the renowned manufactory of Frans Geubels in Brussels underlines their exquisite quality.

Introduction to the Legend of Romulus and Remus

The story of the twin brothers Romulus and Remus, as told in the tapestries of the Kunsthistorisches Museum of Vienna, is based upon a literary source from the time of Augustus. Titus Livius, born in Patavium (today Padua) in 59 BC, was a respected historian in his lifetime and still so in the Renaissance. In his volume of 142 books *Ab urbe condita,* he describes the history of Rome since its founding in 753 BC until the death of Nero Claudius Drusus in 9 BC. Only 35 of his books remain complete, including volume 1 to 10 depicting the mythical founding of Rome and the city's history until 293 BC. It is these volumes which may have inspired the designer of the Vienna tapestries.

The Legend

Proca, a descendant of Aeneas, who had escaped the flames of Troy, ruled the city of Alba Longa in Latium. He bequeathed his throne to his elder son, Numitor. But his younger son, Amulius, overthrew Numitor and occupied the throne. Amulius forced Rhea Silvia, daughter of Numitor, to serve as a priestess to the goddess Vesta so she could not marry and give birth to a rightful heir to the throne. Mars, god of war, however, descended upon

Rhea Silvia and deflowered her. She gave birth to the twins Romulus and Remus. Amulius, when he learned of these events, had Rhea Silvia arrested and ordered the twins to be killed.

The servants, charged to carry out the order, put the twins in a basket in the Tiber river, where the basket was caught by the branches of a fig tree. A she-wolf heard the screams of the children, came to feed them and by this rescued them from death. A shepherd in royal service, Faustulus, discovered the she-wolf, took the twins away from her and raised them with the help of his wife, Larentia. When the twins became young men, they were embroiled in a fight and Remus was caught and brought before Numitor. Faustulus, who suspected from the beginning that he was raising royal heirs, worried much about the twins and revealed to Romulus the long-kept secret. At the same time, Numitor recognized that the posture and character of young Remus did not fit the persona of a servant. The age of Remus and the fact that he had a twin brother, followed by more inquiries, made Numitor realize that Remus was his grandson, whom he had believed to be dead. Remus and Numitor formed an alliance against Amulius and together with Romulus and his shepherds, took action against the king. They succeeded in conquering the palace and killing Amulius. The rightful heir, Numitor, took over to reign.

Out of gratitude, Numitor allowed his two grandsons to found a city in the area where they were found and raised. The brothers started to argue which of them should govern the city and called upon the gods of the location to provide an omen with birds to decide the outcome. Romulus chose the Palatin hill for his place of observation while Remus settled on the Aventin hill. Remus then had the first omen when he saw six vultures, but at the same moment when he wanted to tell his brother, Romulus saw a dozen vultures. Both men were then proclaimed king by their supporters. One side argued for the earlier omen, while the other side for the greater number of the birds observed.

A struggle ensued between the two brothers. Romulus, who was supported by a larger crowd, drew a trench as the border around the future settlement and had a ditch and a small wall built. But Remus derided him and, in mockery, jumped over the still-low border, by which he broke all law and order as city walls were seen as untouchable and holy. Enraged, Romulus killed his brother and said these words: “Anybody will end like this who tries to pass over my walls!”

According to Titus Livius, the newly founded city in 753 BC was governed prudently by Romulus. He declared Rome a free zone and thus it became the refuge for many inhabitants without ties to a particular country. Over time the number of male inhabitants grew steadily, outnumbering the females. Envoys sent to other cities looking for females to expand the growth of Rome were unsuccessful. Romulus, in response, resorted to a ruse by inviting neighboring cities for a festival of combat games. Among the many curious visitors were the Sabines from the adjoining hills. In the middle of the games the Romans plunged into the visiting crowd and caught all the young women they could put their hands on. The other unarmed guests then retreated. After the initial shock was overcome, many of the maidens agreed to marry Romans. The angry male Sabines returned with a strong army to attack the Romans. But the Sabine women intervened and acted as mediators to end the quarrel as they did not want to lose their fathers and brothers on one side and their husbands on the other. Romulus and the ruler of the Sabines, Titus Tatius, shook hands and sealed the peace.

Scenes from the Legend of
Romulus and Remus

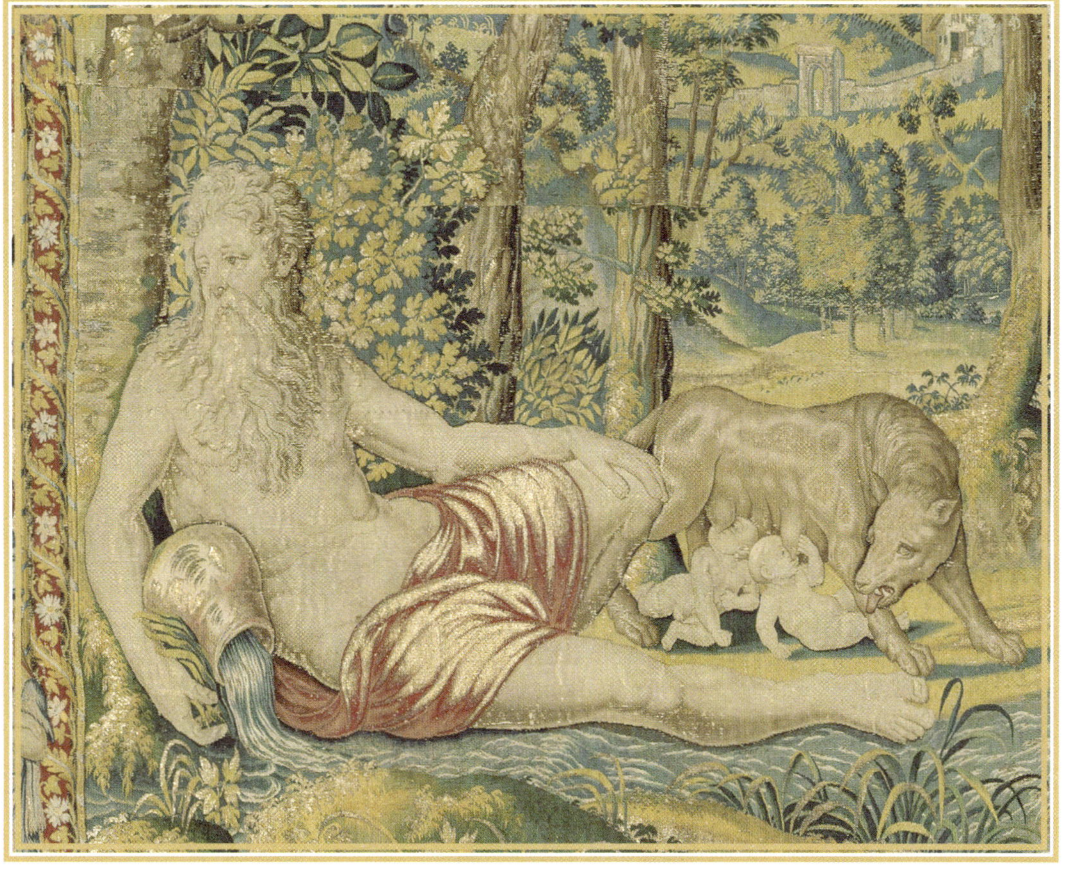

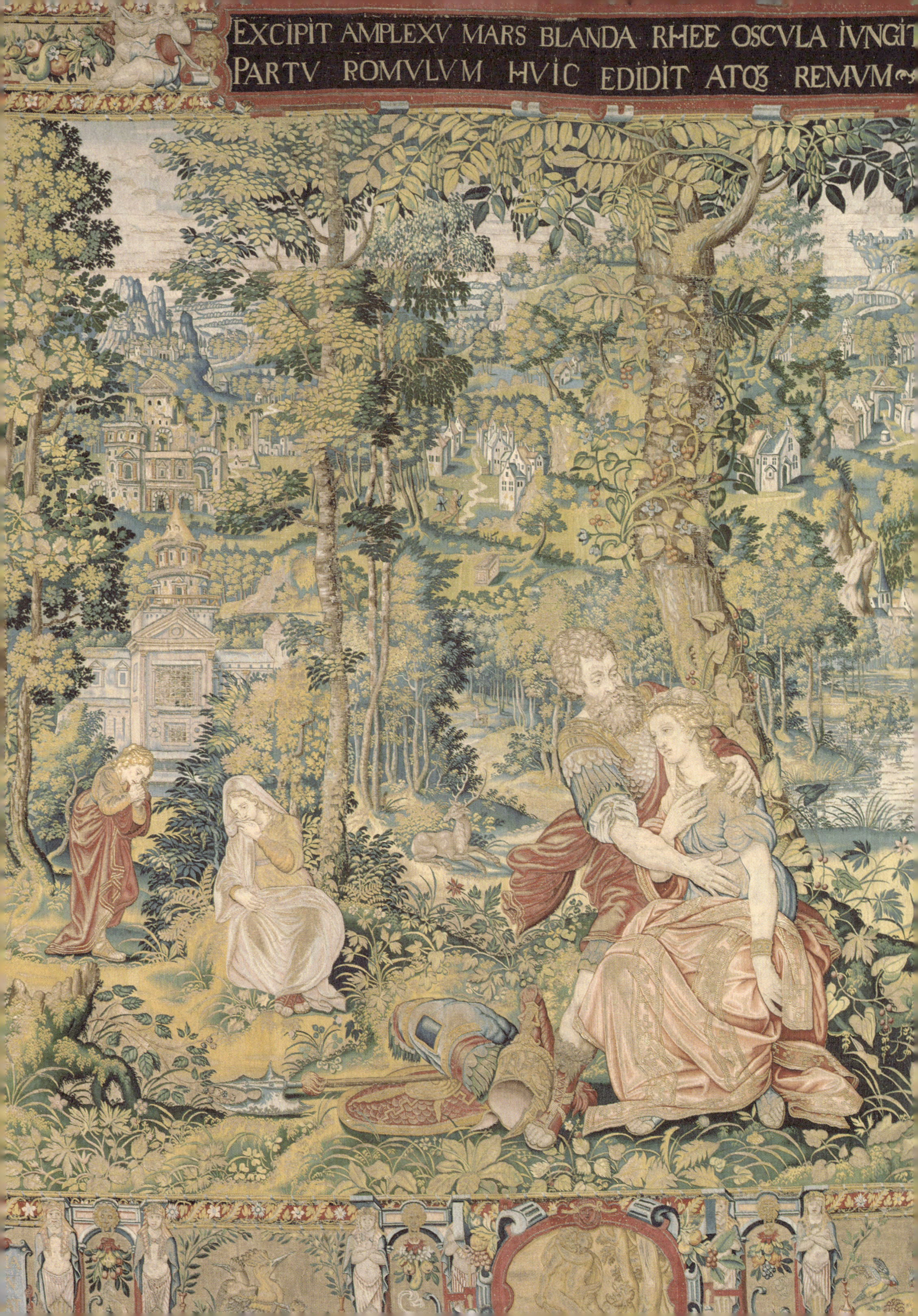
EXCIPIT AMPLEXV MARS BLANDA RHEE OSCVLA IVNGIT
PARTV ROMVLVM HVIC EDIDIT ATQ; REMVM

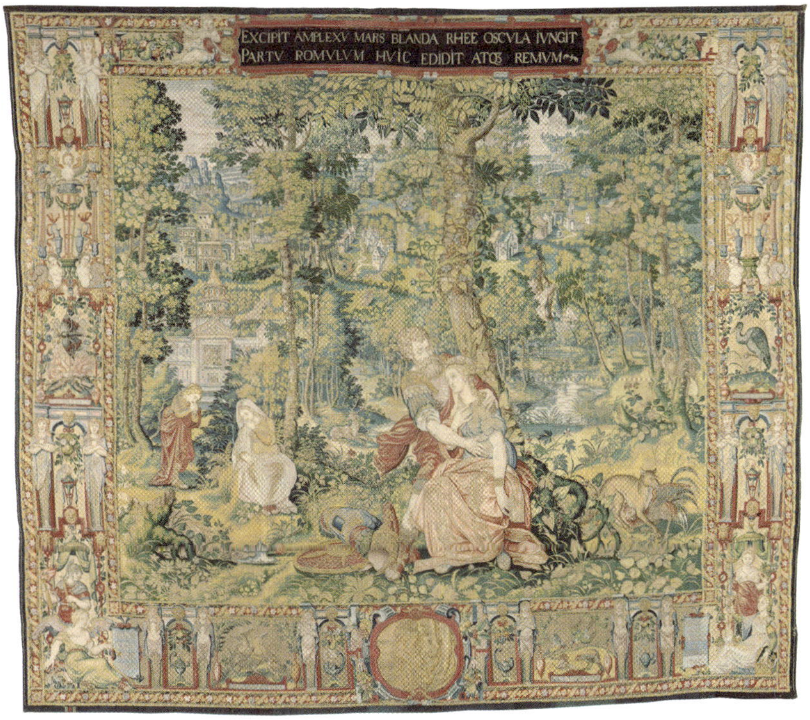

Mars Embraces Rhea Silvia and the Birth of Romulus and Remus

Scenes from the *Saga of Romulus and Remus* series

Brussels, Workshop of Frans Geubels, ca 1560-70

Designer unknown

12 x 13 1/2'

Wool, silk, gold and silver threads

Inscription: EXCIPIT AMPLEXU MARS BLANDA RHEE OSCVLA IVNGIT / PARTV ROMVLVM HVIC EDIDIT ATQUE REMVM

Wien, Kunsthistorisches Museum, Kunstkammer

Mars Embraces Rhea Silvia and the Birth of Romulus and Remus

Preceding the birth of Romulus and Remus was the meeting of Rhea Silvia with Mars, who are depicted in the tapestry's foreground. The seated young woman, dressed in typical classical style, holds her right hand to her breast while her left hand sinks feebly to the ground. This gesture and the empty gaze of her eyes express her defenselessness against the god. In contrast, the god of war stands as an imposing figure next to her. He wears a *lorica squamata* (scale armour), his *clipeus* (round shield), *cassis* (helmet), the *hellebarde* (a cut-and-thrust weapon which is from the 16th century and not from antiquity) and his breast plate, distinguishing him as a god of fighting spirit. With his arms, Mars embraces the submissive Rhea Silvia. His right hand is put on her abdomen, indicating his impending crime. The designer omits the drastic depiction of the rape. Instead, he places the event in an idyllic, lush landscape with a river. A buck, a deer, and a fox that has killed a bird, enliven the scenery. The peacefully grazing and relaxing animals may be seen as a sign of the virginity of Rhea Silvia. But the thieving fox, carrying his victim in his jaws, symbolizes the male superiority of Mars, who took the young woman against her will. The commonly held tradition of depicting scenes happening at different times simultaneously in the same tapestry was still employed in the 16th century. This is illustrated on the left side of the panel where we see Rhea Silvia with her servant after Mars has gone. Ashamed, she bows her head and lifts the cloth to her face, which partly covers her body and blond hair. The cloth and her arms reveal her lower abdomen, which already carries the twins. The servant next to her also bows her head and deplores with folded hands the situation of her mistress. In the background the artists allow the viewer a look through a barred window into the room of a palace-like structure, in which Rhea Silvia is giving birth to the twins.

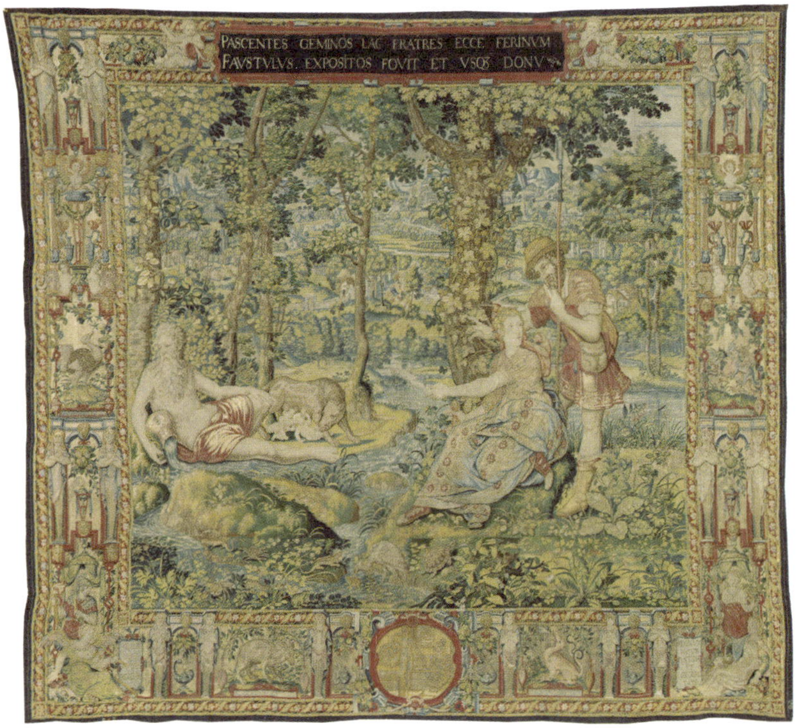

Romulus and Remus are Suckled by the She-wolf

Scenes from the *Saga of Romulus and Remus* series

Brussels, Workshop of Frans Geubels, ca 1560-70

Designer unknown

10 1/2 x 11 1/2'

Wool, silk, gold and silver threads

Inscription: PASCENTES GEMINOS LAC FRATRES ECCE FERINVM / FAVSTVLVS EXPOSITOS FOVIT ET VSQUE DONV

Wien, Kunsthistorisches Museum, Kunstkammer

Romulus and Remus are Suckled by the She-wolf

In the foreground of the second tapestry several of the protagonists stand side by side in equal proportion. These are all the persons involved in rescuing the twins. At the left of the panel the image starts with the personification of the Tiber River, resembling in its composition a Hellenistic sculpture of the Vatican Museum. Tiber is covering his loin only with a red cloth. With his right arm he leans on a jug, emptying itself into the river. Close to him at the banks of the river stands Lupa, the she-wolf, who had found and suckled Romulus and Remus. The two naked foundlings are depicted at the moment when they suckle the teats of the she-wolf. On the opposite side of the river, both Faustulus the shepherd and his wife Larentia are pointing with vivid gestures at the other river bank where Romulus and Remus can be seen. Again, the landscape is idyllic with the panoramic view of a distant city. Along the river bank in the foreground are frogs, lizards, a crab, a turtle and a stork, just having caught a toad. The river banks in the background are left inanimate.

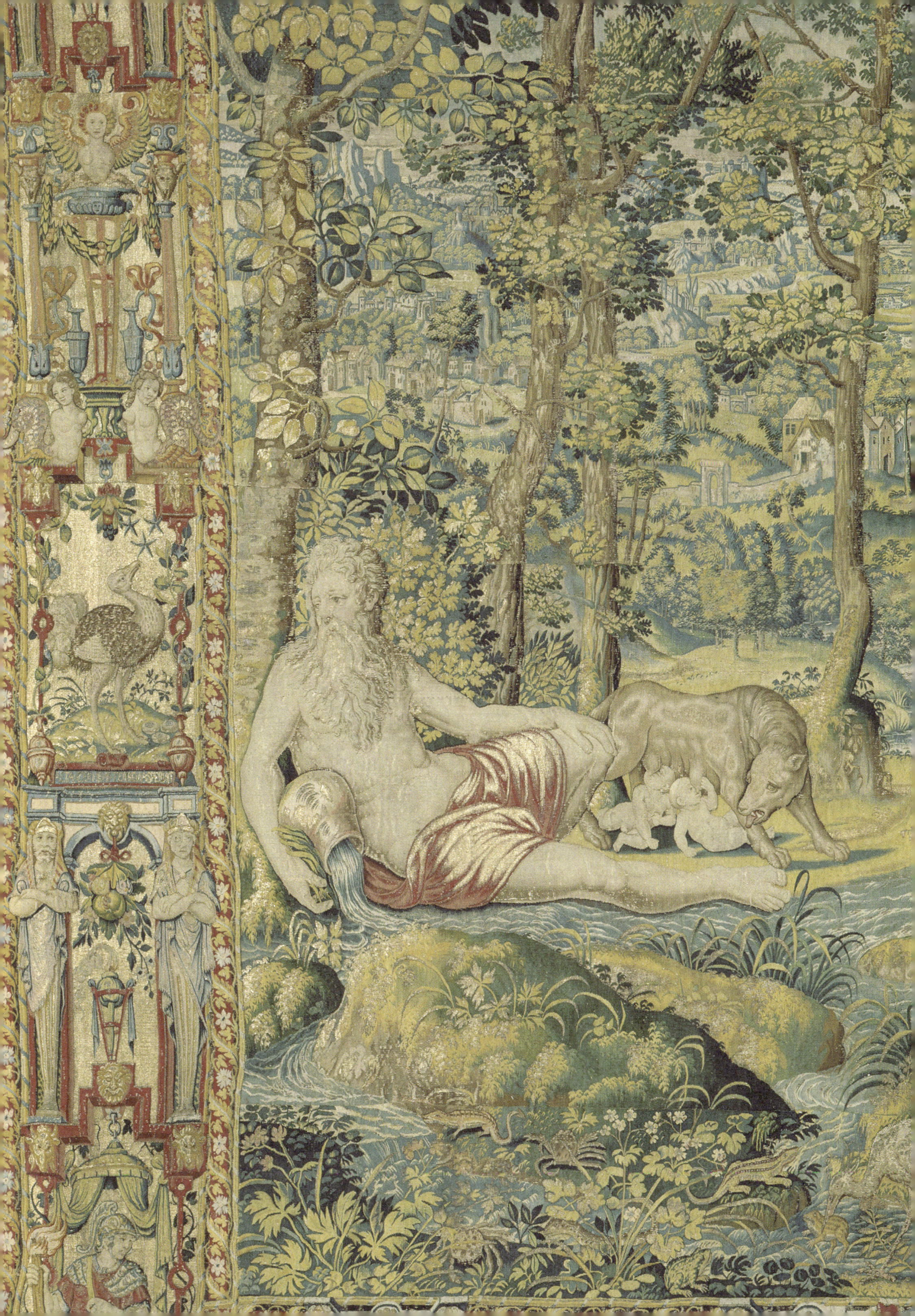

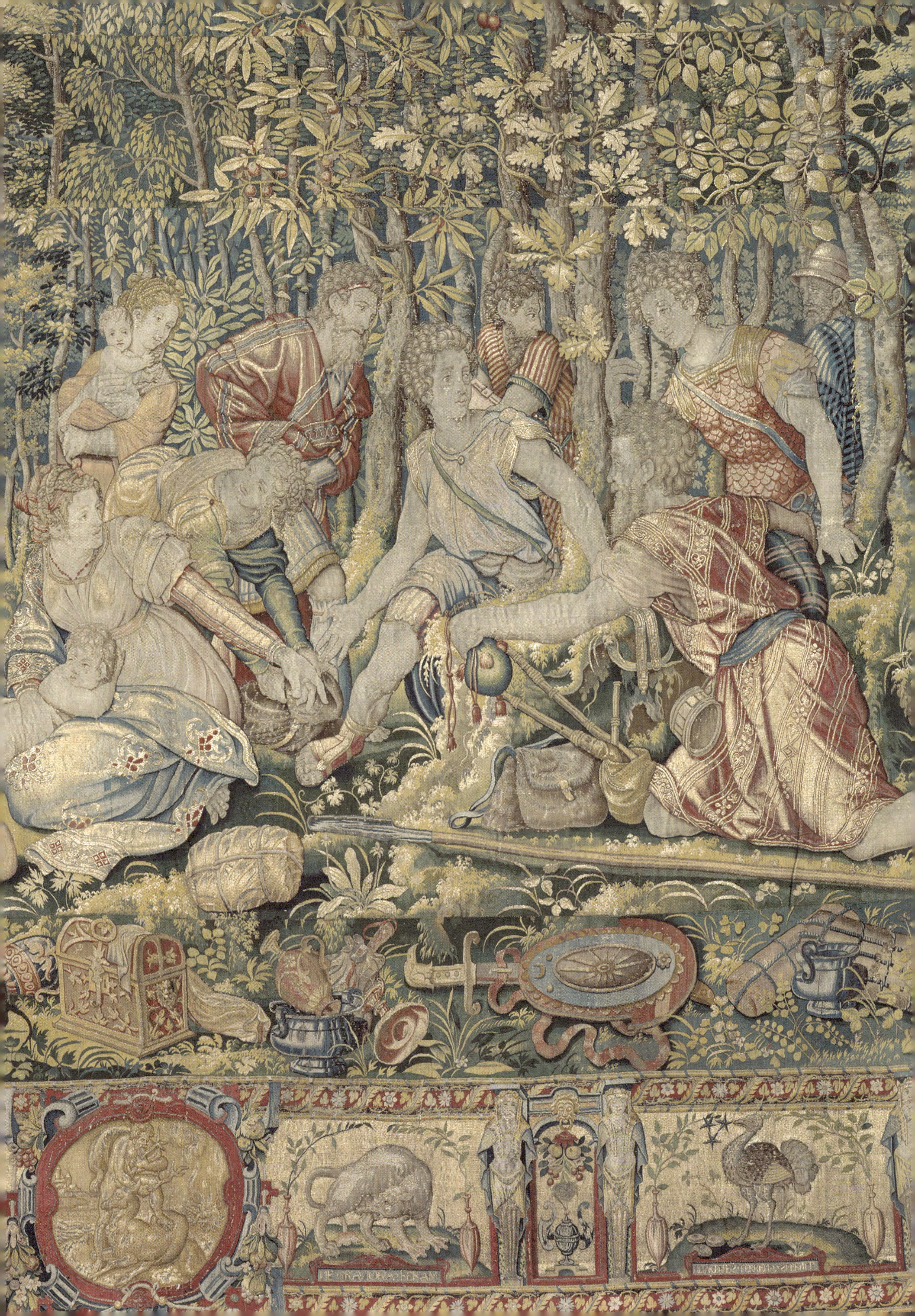

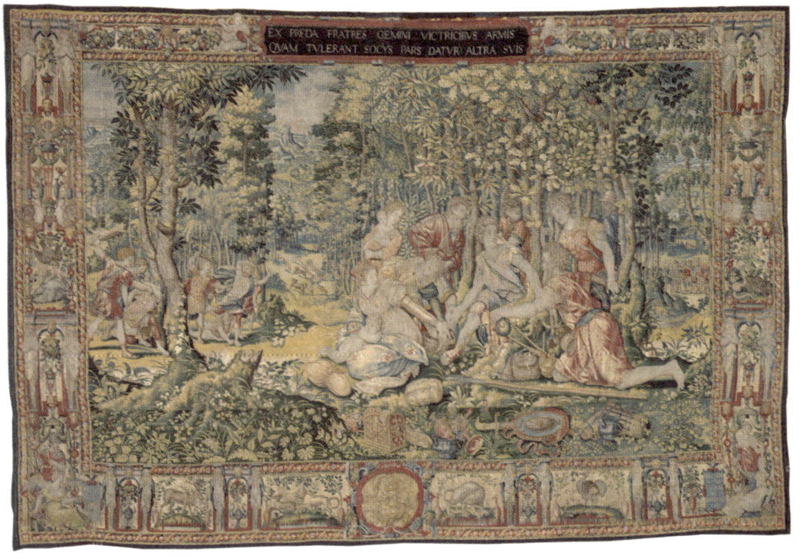

The Twins Sharing the Loot

Scenes from the *Saga of Romulus and Remus* series

Brussels, Workshop of Frans Geubels, ca 1560-70

Designer unknown

11 1/2 x 18 1/2'

Wool, silk, gold and silver threads

Inscription: EX PREDA FRATRES GEMINI VICTRICIBVS ARMIS / QVAM TVLERANT SOCYS PARS DATVR ALTRA SVIS

Wien, Kunsthistorisches Museum, Kunstkammer

The Twins Sharing the Loot

In the developing story, the protagonists are more vividly depicted in this panel than in the two previous panels. According to Livius, the adolescent brothers Romulus and Remus were quite brave. They were devoted to hunting and to being protectors of the shepherds against robbers, whose loot they returned to the victims. Correspondingly, we find two fighting scenes at the left part of the panel, in which the superior party is armed with clubs. Next to it and further back, a hunting scene with dogs is depicted. To the right of the tapestry another combat scene is shown with the capture of the defeated. The main scene in the foreground shows the distribution of repossessed loot. The victorious heroes and two women with their children have met there in a group. Like trophies, objects including jugs, bowls, boxes, tied-up parcels, shield and sword are strewn along the front of the woven image.

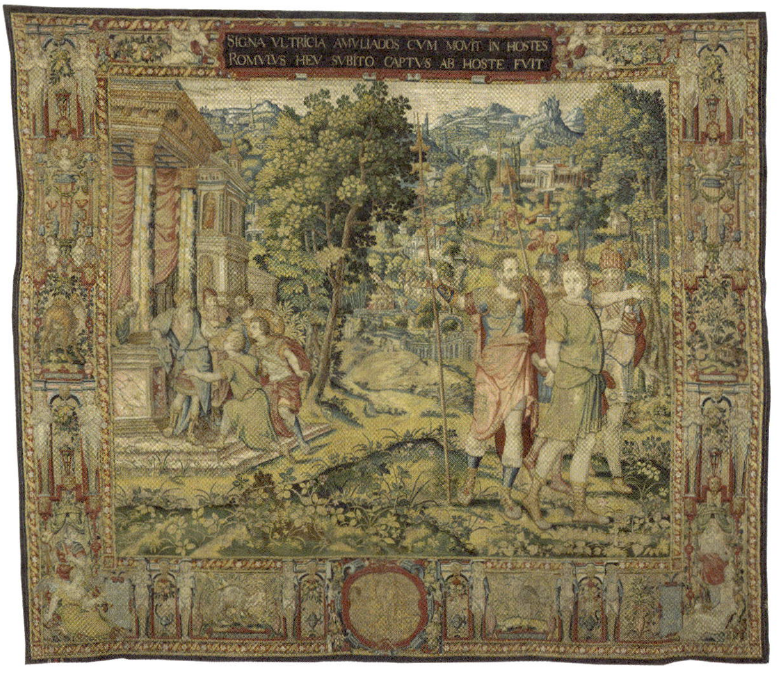

Remus Captured and Brought before Amulius

Scenes from the *Saga of Romulus and Remus* series

Brussels, Workshop of Frans Geubels, ca 1560-70

Designer unknown

11 1/2 x 14 3/4'

Wool, silk, gold and silver threads

Inscription: SIGNA VLTRICIA AMVLIADOS CVM MOVIT IN HOSTES / ROMVLVS HEV SVBITO CAPTVS AB HOSTE FVIT

Wien, Kunsthistorisches Museum, Kunstkammer

Remus Captured and Brought before Amulius

In a struggle, Remus is being captured (the inscription erroneously names Romulus). He is being led away with his hands tied at his back, at the right foreground with a panoramic view of a landscape. Numitor stands on the left in front of an open columned hall. He is surrounded by shepherds of the king who have brought the accusation against Remus. Remus falls on his knees before Numitor with his arms spread in a stirring gesture.

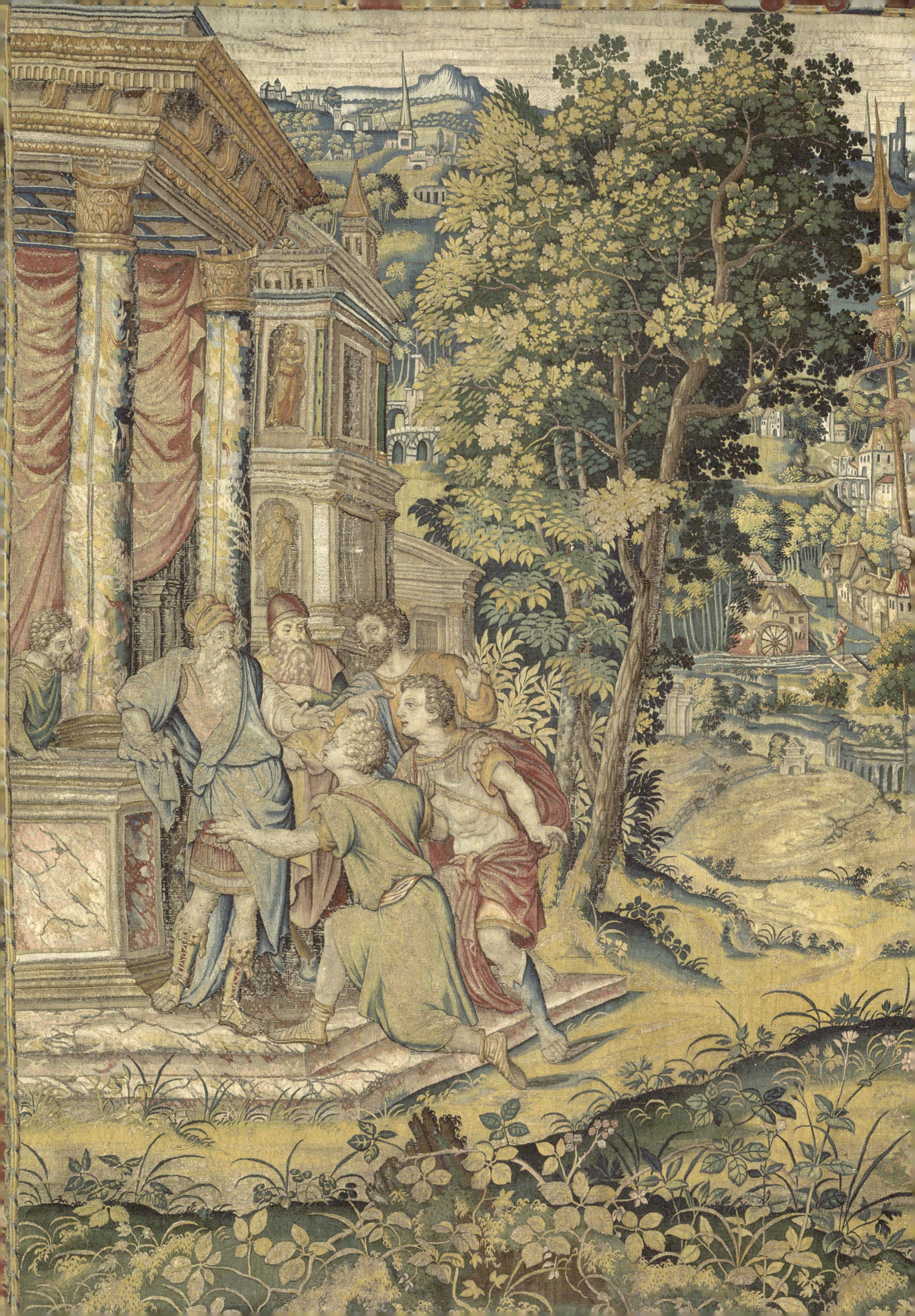

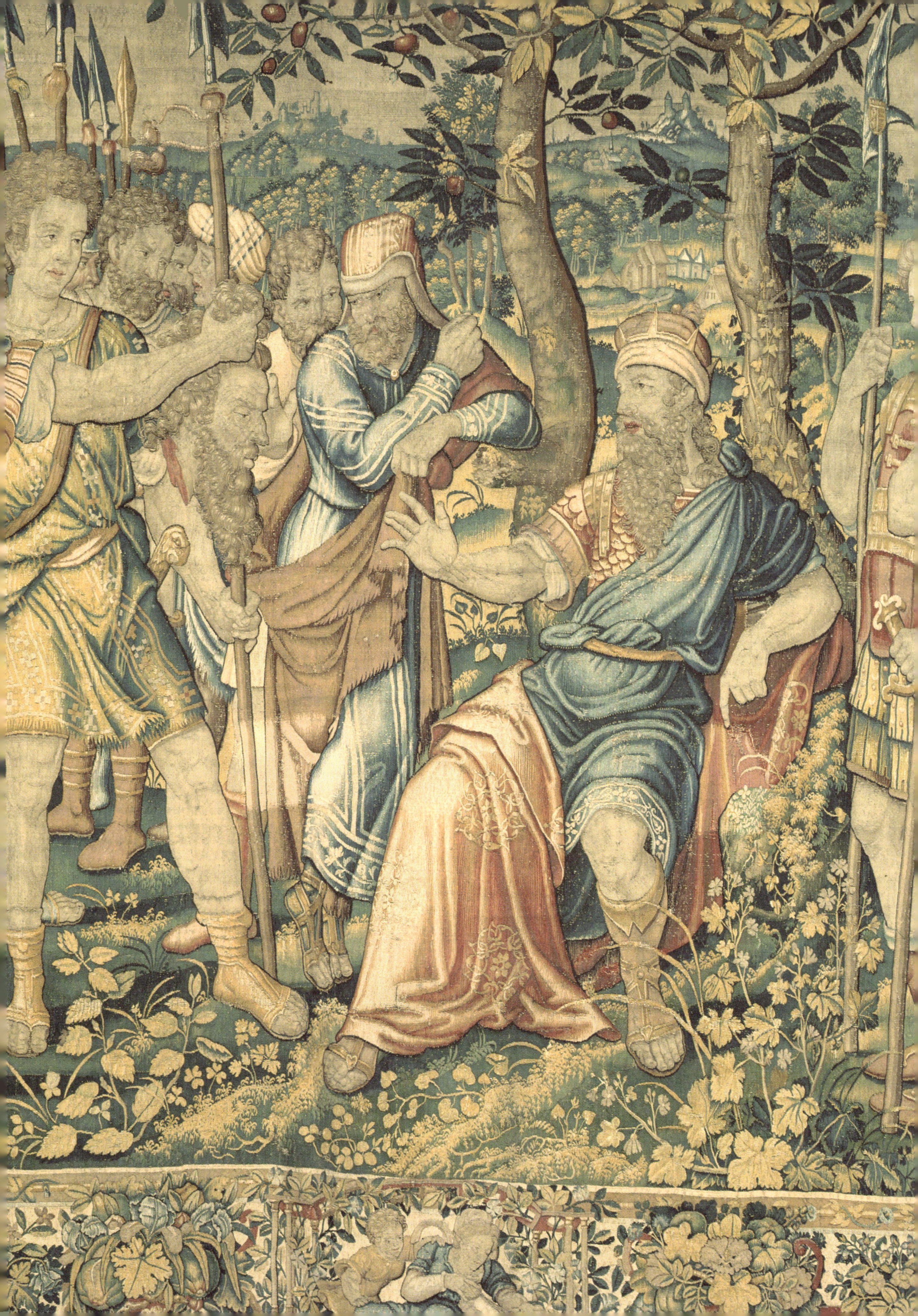

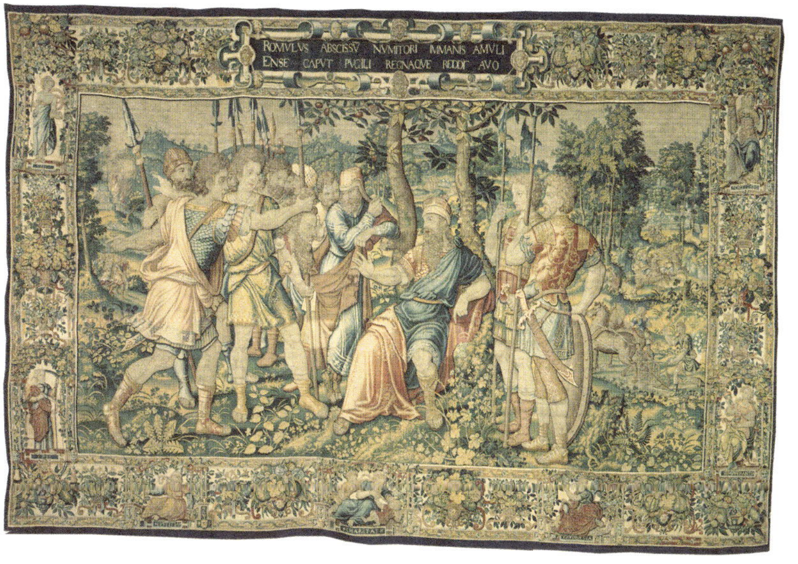

Romulus Delivers the Head of Amulius to Numitor

Scenes from the *History of Romulus and Remus* series

Brussels, ca 1565-70 (no weavers mark)

11 3/4 x 17 1/2'

Wool, silk, gold and silver threads

Inscription: ROMVLVS ABSCISSV NVMITORI IMMANIS AMVLI / ENSE CAPVT PVGILI REGNAQUE REDDIT AVO

Wien, Kunsthistorisches Museum, Kunstkammer

Romulus Delivers the Head of Amulius to Numitor

After Numitor recognized Romulus and Remus as his grandsons, who were believed to be dead, they allied against the unrightful king Amulius to dethrone and kill him. The tapestry here shows Numitor as an old bearded man, seated in the center. With a gesture of his right arm he welcomes Romulus, who is heading toward him to show the head of the defeated Amulius. His brother Remus stands beside him along with shepherds and soldiers who are all surrounded by the same lush landscape as in the other tapestries.

The scene in this tapestry has no direct historical source like the others portrayed in the tapestries, yet it is part of the traditional repertoire to tell the story of Romulus and Remus in the art of tapestry. It is depicted for the first time in a tapestry design by the Flemish painter Bernard van Orley in 1524 (Munich, Graphische Sammlung).

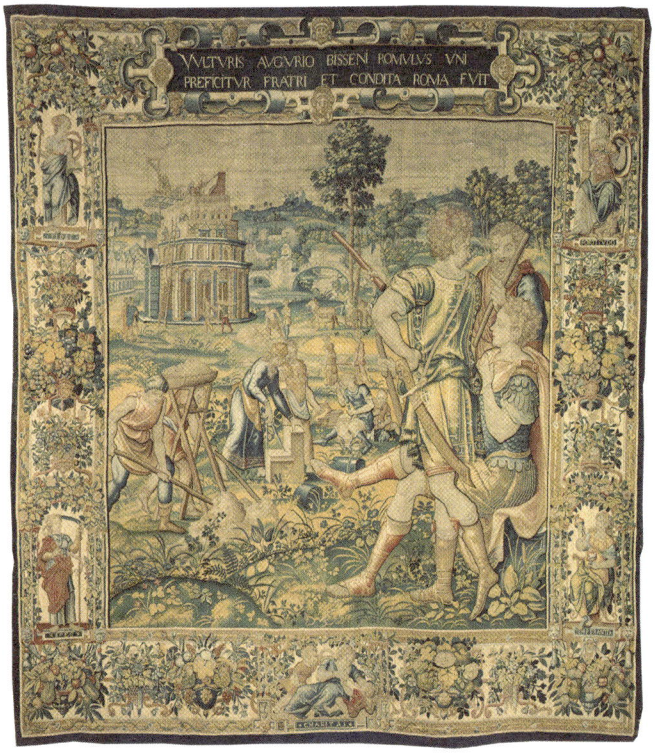

The Founding of Rome

Scenes from the *History of Romulus and Remus* series

Brussels, ca 1565-70 (no weavers mark)

12 x 10 1/2'

Wool, silk, gold and silver threads

Inscription: VVLTVRIS AVGVRIO BISSENI ROMVLVS VNI / PREFICITVR FRATRI ET CONDITA ROMA FVIT

Wien, Kunsthistorisches Museum, Kunstkammer

The Founding of Rome

The victory over Amulius is followed by the legendary bird omen and the fight between Romulus and Remus in which Romulus kills Remus. The gruesome murder of the brother is not shown in the tapestry. The story further unfolds here with Romulus, seated at the right side of this image, listening to the explanations of two architects standing next to him. In the background the city of Rome is being built.

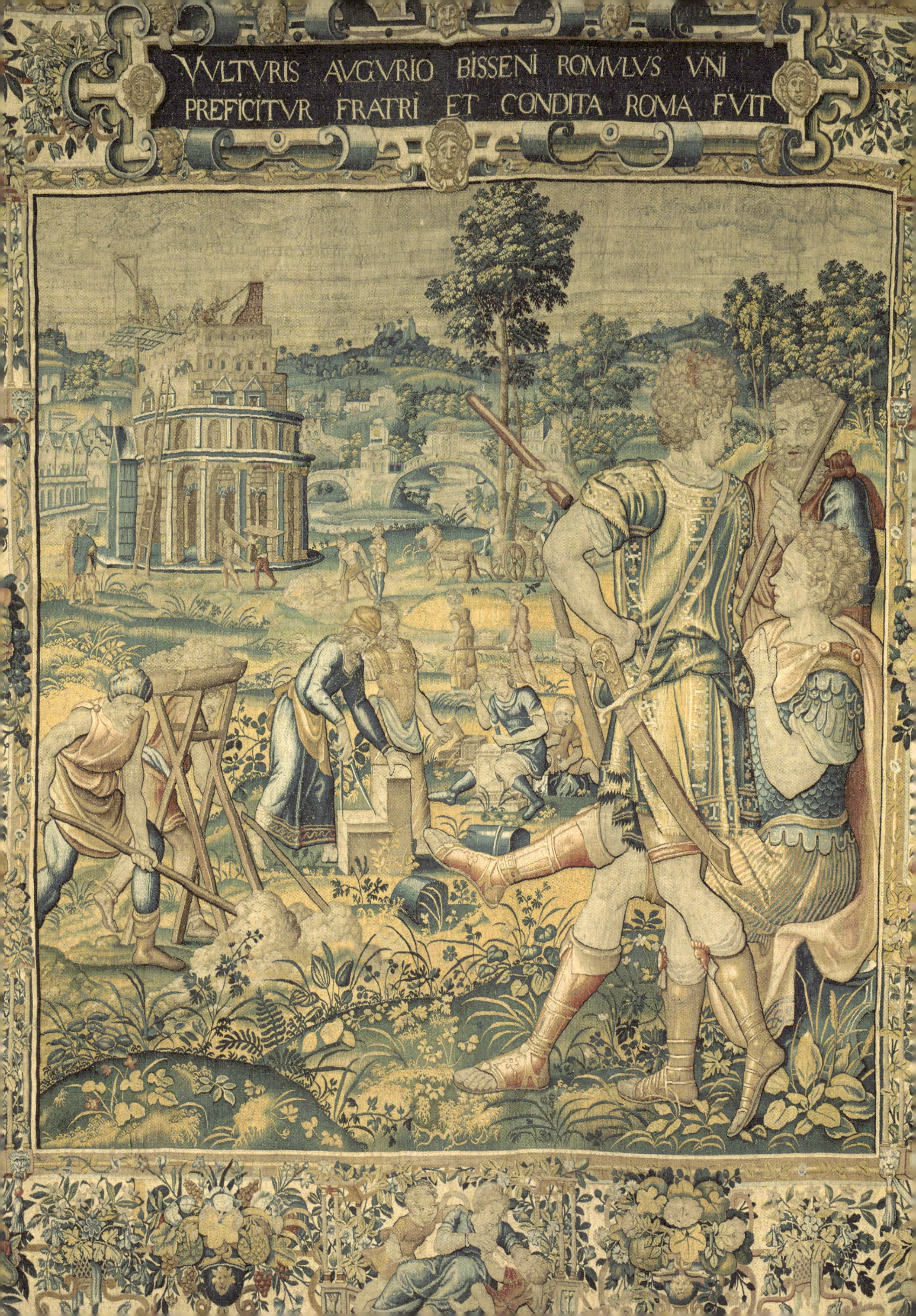
VVLTVRIS AVGVRIO BISSENI ROMVLVS VNI
PREFICITVR FRATRI ET CONDITA ROMA FVIT

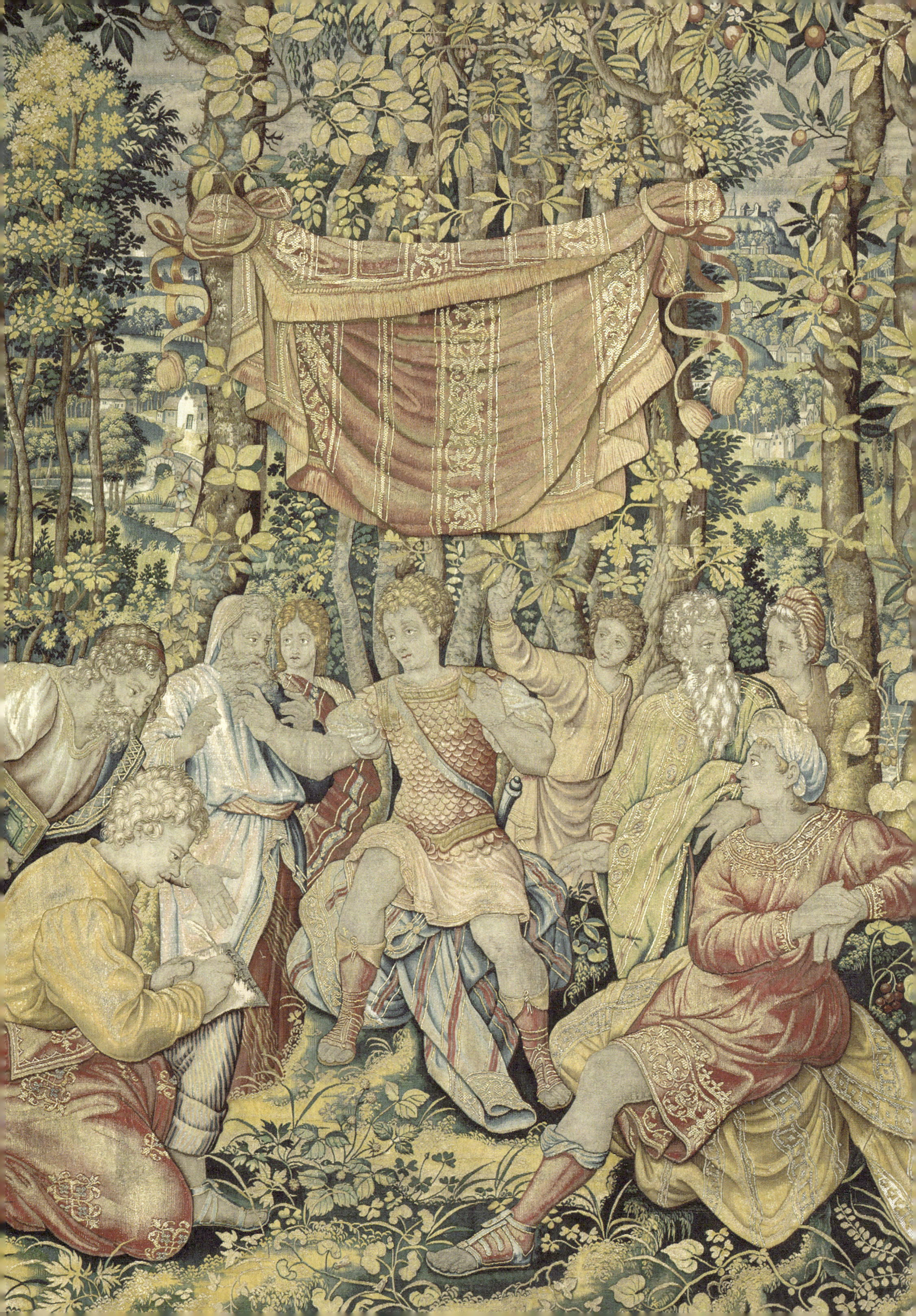

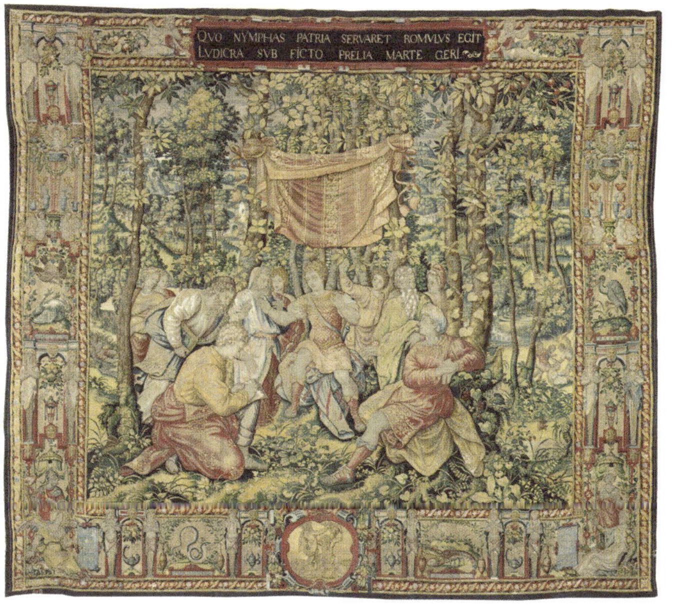

Romulus Invites the Neighbors to the Combat Games

Scenes from the *Saga of Romulus and Remus* series

Brussels, Workshop of Frans Geubels, ca 1560-70

Designer unknown

11 1/2 x 13 1/2'

Wool, silk, gold and silver threads

Inscription: QVO NYMPHAS PATRIA SERVARET ROMVLVS EGIT / LVDICRA SVB FICTO PRELIA MARTE GERI

Wien, Kunsthistorisches Museum, Kunstkammer

Romulus Invites the Neighbors to the Combat Games

When the male population of his new city grows disproportionately to the female population, Romulus resorts to a ruse and invites, among others, the neighboring Sabines to a combat game in Rome. He sits beneath a precious cloth suspended between two trees, as if under a throne canopy in the open landscape. Surrounded by advisors and several women, he dictates the invitation to a scribe kneeling before him. The figure to his right wears an exotic-looking turban on his head.

As a model for the figure motif of Romulus, a tapestry by Raphael can be cited from the famous *Acts of the Apostles* set for the Sistine Chapel (the cartoons are dated 1515/1516). One panel in this series, *The Blinding of the Magician Elymas*, depicts Sergius Paulus in an identical seated motif also with the same posture of the arms.

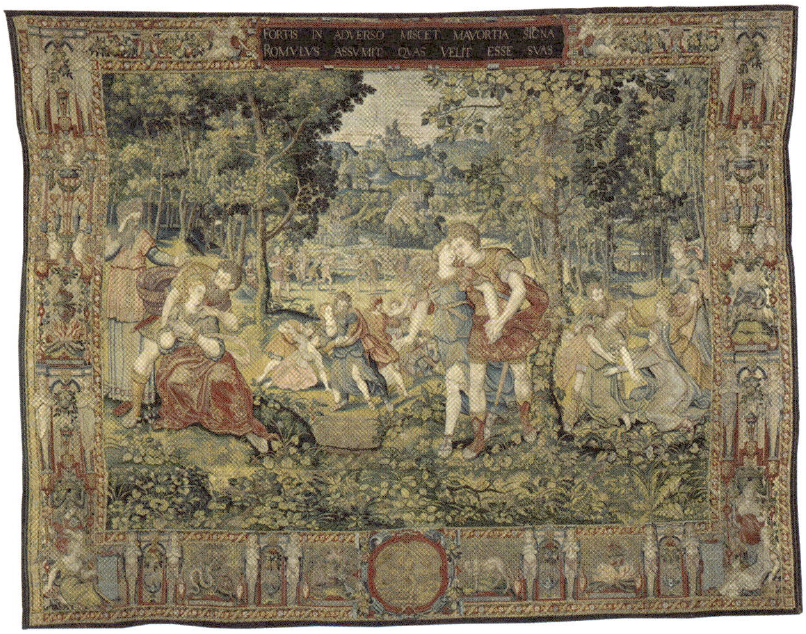

The Rape of the Sabines

Scenes from the *Saga of Romulus and Remus* series

Brussels, Workshop of Frans Geubels, ca 1560

Designer unknown

12 x 15 1/2'

Wool, silk, gold and silver threads

Inscription: FORTIS IN ADVERSO MISCET MAVORTIA SIGNA / ROMVLVS ASSVMIT QVAS VELIT ESSE SVAS

Wien, Kunsthistorisches Museum, Kunstkammer

The Rape of the Sabines

The Vienna tapestry set from the workshop of Frans Geubels depicting the story of Romulus and Remus ends with the rape of the Sabine women. Numerous groups of figures occupy the deep space of landscape with the city of the Sabines on a mountain visible in the background. To the right of the tapestry a Roman grabs a Sabine woman from behind, who defends herself and stretches her arms out toward another woman. A young lady behind her, observing the scene, raises her arms in horror and despair. A couple in the center of the foreground appears almost loving. A Roman walks hand-in-hand with a Sabine woman. His right hand rests on her bosom while she turns her face toward him. More dramatic is the scene to the left of the couple with the assault on other Sabine women. The eight figures at the far left are reminiscent of the composition of Mars and Rhea Silvia in the first panel of the set.

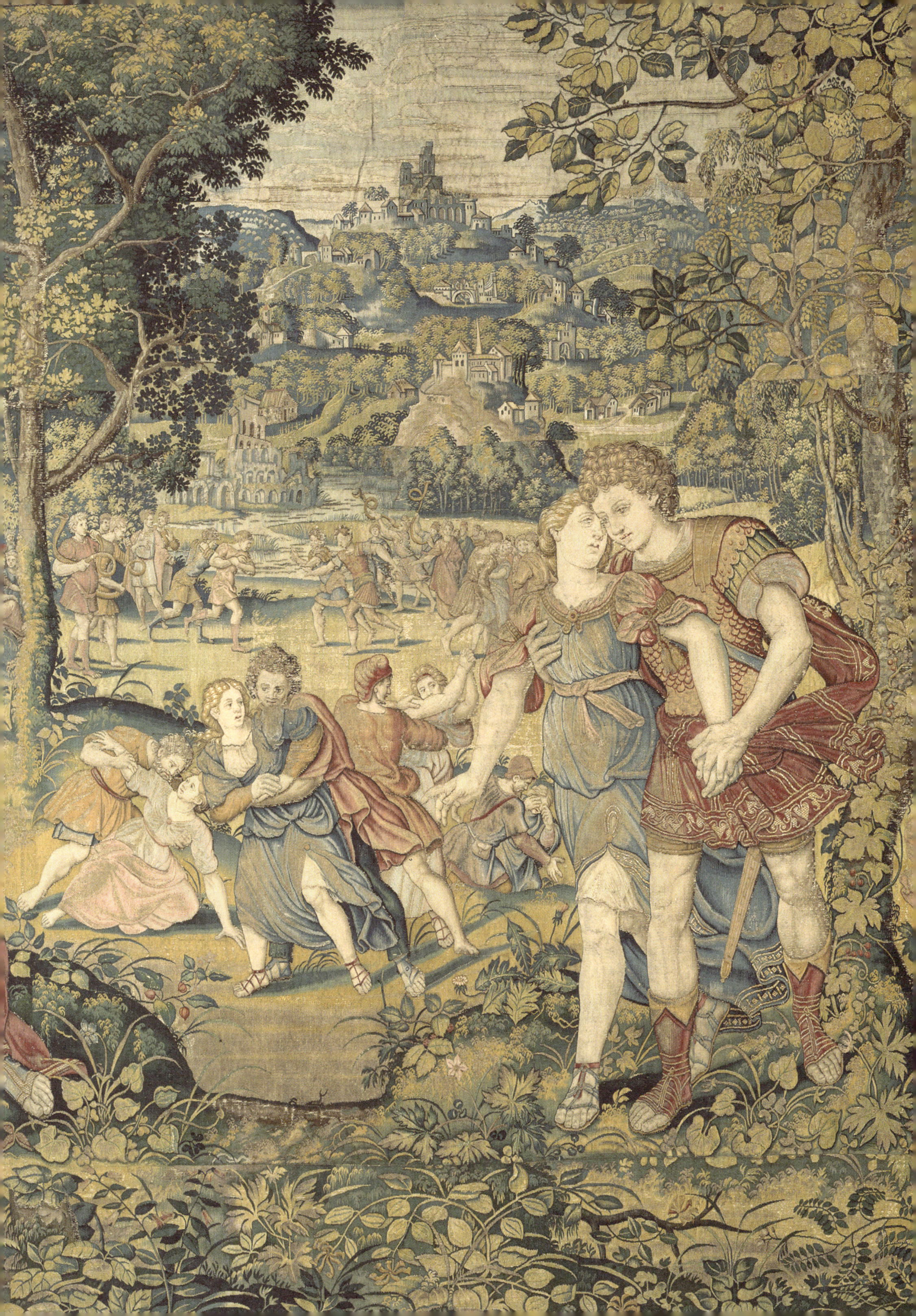

A Hidden Treasure: The Tapestry Collection of Vienna's Kunsthistorisches Museum

After the demise of the Austro-Hungarian monarchy in 1916, the tapestry collection of the Imperial Court was added to the treasure chambers of the Kunsthistorisches Museum (KHM). The collection is impressive not only for its size, some 800 tapestries, but also because of its extraordinary quality and condition. Because of its size, the collection has only been accessible to the general public in small parts of continuously changing displays.

The Middle Ages had already shown tapestries as luxurious works of silk and wool embellished with precious metal threads of gold and silver, which made them costly and time consuming to produce. Despite their mostly monumental sizes, tapestries were extremely fragile objects. Accordingly, they were only displayed temporarily as symbols of dignity and nobility at festive events, or to decorate interiors or public places. Occasionally, rulers took part of their tapestry treasures along with them on voyages. Tapestries were, for example, brought to the Imperial Diets and crowning ceremonies in Prague and Regensburg to adorn the chosen premises adequately. The exceptional tapestry purchases by Emperor Charles V (1500-1558) set a particularly high standard for all other courts of Europe. The earliest recording dates are from 1666 to 1679 when several hundred tapestries were listed, many of which are still in Vienna today. This source, as well as later ones, records the subjects of the tapestries and often the names of the artists and workshops. They can be read like a history of tapestry production from the 16th to the 18th century.

One of the most prominent and outstanding tapestry series in the Vienna collection is the six-panel set of the *History of the King of France*, the so-called *Fontainebleau* series, commissioned by King Francis I for the grand gallery of the castle of Fontainebleau (1540-1550). But how this set found its way to Vienna remains unknown to this day.

Like the *Fontainebleau* series, we have documentation of the ten tapestries of the *Campaigns of Emperor Charles V in Tunis* from 1535. The designs were by Jan Cornelisz Vermeyen and the ten cartoons of 1546-1550. The first edition (*editio princeps*) belongs today to the Patrimonio Nacional in Madrid. Vienna houses the edition of 1712-1721, which were woven after the same cartoons (prepatory drawings) by the Brussels workshop of Jodocus de Vos. Less detailed is the history of the larger part of the Vienna tapestries.

Maximillian II (1527-1576), like his uncle Charles V before him, owned a considerable amount of tapestries. He even had several tapissiers employed solely to take care of his collection. Notable is the series of the *Seven Virtues* by the Brussels workshop of Frans Geubels, which Maximillian inherited from his sister, Queen Katharina of Poland (1533-1572), which are part of the Vienna collection. Many other tapestry series in the collection came from the brother of Maximillian II, the Archduke Ferdinand II of Austria (1529-1595). Archduke Leopold Wilhelm (1614-1662), regent of the Southern Netherlands, was one of the greatest art collectors and patrons among the Habsburg dynasty (1614-1662). Besides having one of the largest collections of paintings, he also had a huge collection of tapestries. In 1652, at the request of Emperor Ferdinand III (1608-1657), he purchased tapestries from Brussels for the court in Prague. Another Habsburg, Emperor Leopold I, also ordered in 1666 an enormous purchase of Flemish tapestries. Leopold was also known for giving away tapestries, including entire sets as gifts.

When Maria Theresia married Franz Stefan von Lothringen in 1736 he brought no less than 20 tapestry series to Vienna. Among these was one exquisite throne-canopy of 1561, as well as *Scenes from the Book of Tobias*, Brussels, 1540-1550, and various hangings with depictions of historic battle scenes.

As gifts to enhance diplomacy, important tapestries were given away by the courts of Europe. In 1777, for example, Marie Antoinette, wife of King Louis XVI, gave her brother, Emperor Joseph II (1741-1790), complete sets of tapestries from the Royale Gobelins Manufactory, when he visited her incognito. (All these tapestries made their way to Vienna.) The last Habsburg to increase the tapestry collection was Emperor Franz Joseph I (1830-1916). He ordered the acquisition of a set of nine tapestries of the *Acts of the Apostles* after Raphael, produced in Brussels around 1600.

The volume of the Vienna tapestry collection has changed time and again during the centuries. Diplomatic presents, purchases and inheritances helped to extend the possessions of the Imperial House. At the same time, losses had to be registered in the form of dowries, gifts to guests, or tapestries given as rewards. Other changes came through losses during wars and a blow suffered in 1992 when two tapestries of a David Teniers series vanished in a fire at the Hofburg in Vienna.

References for Essays:

Thomas P. Campbell, *Henry VIII and the Art of Majesty: Tapestries at the Tudor Court*, New Haven/London 2007, p.195-198

Guy Delmarcel, *Flemish Tapestry from the 15th to the 18th Century*, Tielt, 1999, p. 155-164

Paulina Jonquera de Vega and Concha Herrero Cenretero, *Catalogo de Tapices de Patrimonio Nacional*, Volume I: Siglo XVI, Madrid 1986, p.140-142

Elisabeth Mahl, *Die Renaissance und die Folgen der Tapisserie-Sammlung des Kunsthistorischen Museums*, in: Jahrbuch der Kunsthistorischen Sammlungen in Wien, Bd. 61, 1965, p. 7-40

Checklist

1. *Mars Embraces Rhea Silvia and the Birth of Romulus and Remus*
Scenes from *The Saga of Romulus and Remus* series
ca 1560-70
Brussels, Workshop of Frans Geubels
Warp: wool, weft: wool, silk, silver, and gold
Warp per cm: 7-8 (17 ¾" - 20 ¼")
3.55m x 4.1m (11'8" x 13'5")
Courtesy of Kunsthistorisches Museum, Vienna

2. *Romulus and Remus Suckled by a She-wolf*
Scenes from *The Saga of Romulus and Remus* series
ca 1560-70
Brussels, Workshop of Frans Geubels
Warp: wool, weft: wool, silk, silver, and gold
Warp per cm: 7-8 (17 ¾"- 20 ¼")
3.5m x 3.75m (11'6" x 12'3")
Courtesy of Kunsthistorisches Museum, Vienna

3. *The Twins Sharing the Loot*
Scenes from *The Saga of Romulus and Remus* series
ca 1560-70
Brussels, Workshop of Frans Geubels
Warp: wool, weft: wool, silk, silver, and gold
Warp per cm: 7-8 (17 ¾"- 20 ¼")
3.5m x 5.25m (11'6" x 17'3")
Courtesy of Kunsthistorisches Museum, Vienna

4. *Remus Captured and Brought before Amulius*
Scenes from *The Saga of Romulus and Remus* series
ca 1560-70
Brussels, Workshop of Frans Geubels
Warp: wool, weft: wool, silk, silver, and gold
Warp per cm: 7-8 (17 ¾"- 20 ¼")
3.45m x 4.15m (11'3" x 13'6")
Courtesy of Kunsthistorisches Museum, Vienna

5. *Romulus Delivers the Head of Amulius to Numitor*
Scenes from *The History of Romulus and Remus* series
ca 1565-70
Brussels (no weavers mark)
Warp: wool, weft: wool, silk
Warp per cm: 6-7 (15 ¼" – 17 ¾")
3.5m x 5.3m (11'6" x 17'5")
Courtesy of Kunsthistorisches Museum, Vienna

6. *The Founding of Rome*
Scenes from *The History of Romulus and Remus* series
ca 1565-70
Brussels (no weavers mark)
Warp: wool, weft: wool, silk
Warp per cm: 6-7 (15 ¼" – 17 ¾")
3.61m x 3.24m (11'10" x 10'8")
Courtesy of Kunsthistorisches Museum, Vienna

7. *Romulus Invites the Neighbors to the Combat Games*
Scenes from *The Saga of Romulus and Remus* series
ca 1560-70
Brussels, Workshop of Frans Geubels
Warp: wool, weft: wool, silk, silver, and gold
Warp per cm: 7-8 (17 ¾"- 20 ¼")
3.45m x 4.1m (11'4" x 13'5")
Courtesy of Kunsthistorisches Museum, Vienna

8. *The Rape of the Sabines*
Scenes from *The Saga of Romulus and Remus* series
ca 1560-70
Brussels, Workshop of Frans Geubels
Warp: wool, weft: wool, silk, silver, and gold
Warp per cm: 7-8 (17 ¾"- 20 ¼")
3.55m x 4.75m (11'8" x 5'7")
Courtesy of Kunsthistorisches Museum, Vienna